The Supernatural

Haunting Tales of Lucknow

The Supernatural

Haunting Tales of Lucknow

PC Sarkar

KALPAZ

Published by

Kalpaz Publications
C-30, Satyawati Nagar,
Delhi – 110052
Ph.: 011-47034999, 9811692060
www.kalpazpublications.com
E-mail: kalpaz@hotmail.com

Distribution Network
www.gyanbooks.com
India, USA, Canada, UK, Australia, France

ISBN: 978-93-5722-425-3 (HB)
First Published, 2025

Printed at: Gyan Press, Delhi.

The Supernatural
Haunting Tales of Lucknow
Author: PC SARKAR

Lucknow Residency Cemetery (1860), Francis Frith

Contents

"What you seek is seeking you"

- Rumi

"Do not call up that which you cannot put down"

- HP Lovecraft

Prologue

Among the things that go bump in the night, there are ghosts, ghouls, werewolves, vampires, zombies, poltergeists and other assorted demonic entities from the spirit world, which have been stalking mankind since time immemorial. These are mostly malevolent in nature, although the benevolent dead have also been reported. In fact, not all are disembodied spirits, or souls of people who were once alive. Several entities can be elementals, who are not full fledged souls but low forms in the spirit world which can create trouble, but are quite powerless to cause actual physical harm. Poltergeists are mischievous supernatural beings that throw things around, but generally cause no serious damage. Then there are tree spirits, water spirits, fairies, goblins and such like. It has been reported that there are “thought spirits” which are the products of our thoughts; these emerge from our navels, and can be friendly or inimical, depending on the kind of thought process that created them. In the realm of the supernatural - fact, fantasy, the real and the unreal become a formidable mix. This mix is powered by us humans who may possess ESP (extra sensory perception), enabling us to detect the entities of the spirit world and even converse with them. There are mediums, who can summon the souls of dead people; often mediums are aided by a “guardian spirit” or “spirit guide.” Ouija Boards and planchettes aid in automatic writing, enabling the dead to communicate with the living, although the technique can be quite tedious and prone to give erroneous results. Clairvoyants have a “sixth sense” which they use to predict the future and also to earn a living. There are crystal gazers who can predict the future by gazing into a crystal ball; others do the same thing by “reading” patterns of tea leaves. Palmists read palms; faith healers heal people without the use of medicine and surgery. There were witches, wizards and warlocks, particularly in the dark Middle Ages, who worshipped the Devil and obtained powers, thereby obtaining material wealth and / or political clout. Although in recent times, the practice of witchery and wizardry is proudly admitted as being the practice of *wicca*, a modern earth-centric religion, with pagan origins. It must be acknowledged, however, that such an admission in the Middle Ages would have resulted in being burnt at the stake at the cross-roads of the town / village concerned. But then, those were the dark ages. Ours is a lighter age, where everything is permissible and conviction can be extremely difficult. Even for the most heinous of crimes, including mass-murderers. Practitioners of the Left Hand Path are so called because they worship the various forms of the Devil, or to be succinct, are Devil Worshippers or Black Magicians. Similarly, practitioners of the Right Hand Path are followers of a righteous God, and hence practice White Magic. Many do no accept this premise, stating that Lucifer, a product of Christian theology was himself an Angel, before he was cast out of heaven. That the powers of Light and the powers of Darkness are equal and there is a constant war between them, with neither emerging as the victor. Hence, the hours of daylight are equal to that of darkness, and the unfortunate human being is just grist for this mill of these two superpowers.

The above discussion should not give the wrong impression that supernatural beings and supernatural phenomenon have mainly emerged from the western world or Christian beliefs. No sir. All cultures, ancient and modern have their share of folklore, with a definite positioning for gods, demons, various supernatural beings and their activities. Sometimes gods also become ferocious or vengeful and cause harm to humans, thereby blurring their godliness in such instances. The knowledgeable priest then applies his knowledge to assuage the anger of that particular god and minimise the losses. In the same way that an exorcist cleanses a human being possessed by an evil spirit or demon, but sometimes, the damage caused is irreversible, both for the possessed and the exorcist. There seems to be a strict regimentation or delegation of powers in the supernatural world, and strangely, this demarcation is based on what we humans have theorised throughout the ages. For example, the Hindu *tantrik* cannot tackle a Jewish demon or *dybbuk* with his *mantras* (chants). Similarly, a Christian priest's evocations and intonations will have no effect on an Indian (=read Hindu) evil spirit or *rakshasa*. Or on *Pazuzu*, an ancient demon described in Mesopotamian texts. Hindu theology has the *devta/deva* or god and the *asura* or demon. But *asuras* also worship the same god and get formidable powers if the god in question is pleased and decides to be benevolent. This complicates the eternal conflict between the *devas* and the *asuras*. Islam too has its share of demons and creatures from the netherworld, which only the practising Muslim holy man can address. This includes *Iblis*, who is equivalent to the Christian *Satan*, who is actually Lucifer discussed above. Satan is also equivalent to *Shaitan* in Hindu demonology. *Jinns* (*djinns*) and *ifrits* are other demonic entities in Islamic theology. And what about Buddhism, which is another great religion of the world, with a substantial follower base? The demon *Māra* initially manifested as a messenger, delivering the alarming news that Devadatta had seized the Śākya throne from Gautama's lineage. Subsequently, Māra unleashed a tremendous tempest characterized by rain, rocks, ashes, and darkness, which caused all the deities assembled to pay tribute to the future Buddha to flee in fear. *Yōkai* (strange apparition) are a class of supernatural entities appearing in Japanese folklore. The Chinese have their own *gui* or disembodied spirits, who can become demons in the long run. Other demons of Chinese origin (I am serious here) include the *chiyou* and the *gonggong*. Sometimes, two or more religious beliefs get combined and the results can be horrendous. For example, in Haiti (a small island country, south of the Bahamas), the locals worship a strange combination of gods from Roman Catholicism as well as from local West African heritage. Thus, the *Houngan* or priest worships the Loa who are a collection of African Gods and Roman Catholic saints. This religious practice is called *Voodoo*. Quaint as they may seem, voodoo practices can he horribly potent; one of the offshoots of this is the ceremony of reviving the dead, who become *zombies*, discussed later. Then, there are *kobolds*, who guard the depths of our coal mines, but they can be placated by offerings of food and water. *Banshees* utter a scream as a premonition of death in the family, to which they are spiritually attached.

Thus, we see that a discussion on gods, demons, ghosts and spirits can be endless, and somewhat pointless. Occasionally hilarious, and sometimes truly frightening. We also have to take into consideration the various cinema tropes (which leave everlasting impressions on our psyche), in which demons crawl on ceilings and rotate their heads; they spew vomit and hurl choice epithets and abuse. Demons can cause blood to flow from taps, doors to slam, furniture to move, utensils to collect grime, balls to bounce on their own - the list is endless. Zombies shuffle along and eat nothing but human brains. They are pretty dumb and can be shot "dead" by simple guns. Vampires are dressed nattily - mostly ermine-lined long coats for the males and deep cut blouses exposing bulging cleavages, together with flouncy skirts for the females. They suck blood, but they also grant a kind of eternal life to their prey, preferably pretty girls, again with bulging cleavages. They can be destroyed by sunlight and are frightened (but not destroyed) by garlic and crucifixes. They can be "killed" when asleep in their coffins (in the basements of castles) by driving a wooden stake through their hearts. *Werewolves* in Europe and the *Weretigers* of India are normal humans during day time, but become extremely ferocious man-eaters at night, after the full moon rises. They can be subdued by silver bullets though, while they look up and howl at the moon.

Aside from the presence of demonic entities, what motivates ordinary humans to "return" to the realm of the living as "ghosts" following their death? There are several straightforward explanations for this phenomenon. The first explanation is that the person after dying is not really aware that he is dead. As a disembodied spirit, he can observe his mortal remains and even attend his own funeral. He is perplexed as to what actually happened to him and tends to wander about in his former world, sometimes even trying to communicate with the living, but not succeeding. In the case of a murder or war, he might be doomed to "relive the event" again and again till such time his "memory" survives. Eventually, he may be led away to the land of the dead or spirit world, or higher astral plain by benevolent entities (which may include the spirits of those who had loved him during his life time). This "lost spirit" phenomenon occurs particularly during sudden deaths like accidents or even murder. The second type of wandering spirit can be of a human who had an excessive attachment for worldly possessions and physical comforts, including riches and even sex. These spirits are unable to "let go" and remain earth-bound for quite some time and can even cause trouble for the living. The third type of earth bound spirits belong to the "revenge" category - people who have faced some kind of injustice during their lifetimes and want to inflict some sort of revenge on the person or persons who troubled them in life. These vengeful spirits can be malicious and often, in their anger and desire for revenge, the results of their activities may have adverse effects. To put in simple words, their lack of intelligence and overpowering desire for revenge may result in their attacking the wrong person(s) and creating more problems for the living as well as the dead person himself. Such malicious spirits also try to possess human bodies to give a physical angle to their revenge tactics. Needless to say, nobody benefits from all this in the long run; not the human concerned, and certainly not the spirit, as it may be barred from entering a higher astral plain due to its negative actions. The last kind of wandering spirit is one which tries to communicate something urgent to the living before "passing on." A secret or the location of a document, or some hidden asset (=read money) or even some strategy, which the spirit feels is essential to be known to the living. Once the information is successfully passed on, the spirit moves on. But this is easier said than done. The spirit world does not have a time line corresponding to the time line of the living world. Sometimes centuries may pass and generations of the living might come and go, and yet the wandering spirit tries to unsuccessfully communicate with the living. Such wandering spirits constitute the maximum number "ghosts" recorded in history.

It has been surmised that the so-called spirits actually exist in a realm which is quite different from ours. This is actually another phase called "etheric", which is a kind of electric medium. Entities sometimes run out of the energy which enables them to exist there and carry on their activities. Then they "steal" energy from the physical world, often from electrical power sources, energies generated during sexual activity, from hyperactive children and / or adolescents or simply a sleeping human being (I may have experienced the last, but more of that later). Since supernatural entities are powered by a sort of electrical energy discussed above, modern day "ghost-busters" or "ghost hunters" hold a strong belief that such entities can be detected, captured and even disposed off by the use of specialised electrical (and now electronic) equipment like EMF meters, digital video cameras, thermo-graphic and night vision cameras, "ghost traps" and assorted paraphernalia.

So where does all this discourse on the supernatural leave us now? And what is the Lucknow connection? Actually, the city of Lucknow has always been steeped in history and continues to bear the tag of being a heritage city, even though it is as contemporary as any other metropolitan city of the country. But then again, it is not unusual that this city, with a tragic history of wars, massacres, mass executions and hurriedly buried dead bodies, (often without proper rites or graves), during 1857 should have several accounts of supernatural haunting. At least three sites in the city saw heavy casualties on both sides, that is, the British soldiers and the Indian freedom fighters in 1857 - 58. These include the *Residency*, the *Sikandar Bagh* and the *Begum Kothi*. These were reputed to be haunted, together with other sightings (Sarkar, 2015). But all ghostly phenomena are not confined to sites of bloody warfare. Ghostly activity can also happen in a modern day apartment complex. However, it is another matter that the apartment might have been illegally built by an unscrupulous real estate developer over a former, disused graveyard.....

This book is a collection of short stories and one novella (most appropriately 13 in number), based on the supernatural happenings in Lucknow. Although there are several books of this genre, based on cities like Delhi, Calcutta (Kolkata), Bombay (Mumbai) and even places like Goa or Shimla, there has been no serious attempt to produce a similar work on Lucknow till date. My earlier books on the lost heritage of Lucknow (Sarkar 2015, 2023) had fleetingly described such phenomena, leaving my readers clamouring for more. The present work can be described as a work of "historical fiction" - the historical part being meticulously researched and presented, after thorough checks and counter-checks for the sake of accuracy, and then the narrative part, which has its origins from urban legends and local folklore. Since the latter are hazy, they have been embellished by the author, using a degree of artistic or creative license, to make the narrative interesting enough to be presented in a book form for the average reader, who may or may not be a historian or a hard core heritage enthusiast.

People often ask me if I have personally experienced any supernatural phenomenon or ghostly activity, since I spend a lot of time among ruins, cemeteries and derelict structures across the country and even abroad, in pursuit of my rather morbid hobby. I will therefore narrate one unexplained incident, which was not in any ruin but in a modern apartment complex (not in Lucknow), where I was residing about ten years ago. One night I was unable to sleep. When sleep finally came, it was a very restless one. Half-way through the night, I felt an enormous weight on me, as if someone was sitting on my chest and sucking out my vitals. The uneasy, claustrophobic feeling continued all through the night, as I tossed and turned but could get no relief. The next morning, I had a morning flight to board for Delhi. My wife had already left for her school and breakfast was on the table. Feeling weak and nauseous, I decided to skip breakfast at home and go to the open balcony for some fresh air, before leaving for the airport, where I could breakfast. From the balcony, looking below, I saw the preparations on for a funeral. The tenant residing in the apartment below mine, a venerable old man, had died during the night. I regret to state that we had not enjoyed a very cordial relationship, when he was alive, mostly because of car parking issues.

To cut a long story short, I left for the airport, feeling fresh and healthy within minutes of the cab leaving the apartment complex and the accompanying gloom enveloping the area. So had I experienced a ghostly phenomenon during the night, when there was a corpse lying just below my bedroom, and we were separated by merely one floor? Was the old man, now no longer a human, moving around in my apartment, oblivious to the fact that he had to respect human privacy? And was he trying to suck out the energy from my vitals, either for his own survival or as a form of revenge or resentment? Or was it just my overwrought imagination? I leave it to the reader to decide.

So here's to chills, thrills and sleepless nights!!

Mahanagar, Lucknow **PC SARKAR**

March, 2025

Moonlight and Roses

> *"Imagine courts as large as the Temple Gardens, surrounded by ranges of palaces, or at least of buildings well stuccoed and gilded, with fresco-paintings here and there on the blind-windows, and with green jalousies and Venetian blinds closing the apertures which pierce the walls in double rows. In the body of the court are statues, lines of lamp-posts, fountains, orange groves, aqueducts, and kiosks with burnished domes of metal..."*
>
> - William Howard Russell (1858), *The Times*, London

Radha Rani was thrilled with her new home in the heart of erstwhile Nawabi Lucknow. On the verge of womanhood, the young princess was no stranger to life in a palace. But her estate of Naraingarh in the hinterlands of erstwhile Awadh was so *remote.* And also *rustic.* Post 1857, Radha's father, Raja Shivamber Singh had been honoured by no less than Lord Canning himself, together with other *ta'aluqdars*, or landed barons. The canny (pun intended) Governor General (later as the first Viceroy of British India) and his advisors had come across this shrewd plan of creating a buffer zone of nobility between the British Government and the common people of erstwhile Awadh, since the old Nawabi order could no longer be trusted to be loyal to British interests. During the uprising of 1857 - 1858, most *ta'aluqdars* had sided with the freedom fighters, while a lesser number had preferred to support the British, due to their own personal compulsions. Few, like Raja Man Singh (referred to as *Maun Sing* by the British) preferred to run with the hares and hunt with the hounds, so that no one was really clear as to whose side he was on.

After the rebellion was suppressed, the victorious British, on first thoughts, were inclined to raze the Kaiserbagh palace complex to the ground, because of its association with the freedom fighters and their intrepid leader, Begum Hazrat Mahal. When the flush of victory subsided and sanity prevailed, it was decided to hand over the area to the loyal *ta'aluqdars*, and encourage them to settle in Lucknow. On the other hand, the rebellious leaders were hounded, killed and their properties confiscated. The *sanad* or land grant to the *ta'aluqdars* explicitly mentioned that the Kaiserbagh palaces would have to be maintained properly, without any modifications, leasing out or sale being totally prohibited. However, by this time, Kaiserbagh was already in ruins, having been vandalised and partially destroyed by marauding, rampaging British, Sikh and Gorkha soldiers. To quote Russell again, this time in 1859:

"What is to be done with the Kaiserbagh? A mere shell is all that now remains of rows of palaces. The wind whistles as it lists through unglazed windows and shattered Venetians - through door-less corridors and battered walls. The gardens still remain, but the fountains have ceased to play; the statues - marble and plaster - are all gone. The grand mausoleum of Saadat Ali, the last wise and good Nawab who reigned over Oude, is closed, and the ruin of cannon shot and shell is aggravated by the unresisted effects of rain and wind. A few of the buildings are used as quarters, but by far the greater portion of the palaces of the Kaiserbagh is untenanted."

Kaiserbagh had been playground of Wajid Ali Shah, the last king of Awadh. The palace complex housed numerous *kothis* (mansions), where the king, his begums (queens) and the nobility had resided. In addition to that, it housed the *Pari Khana* or House (Abode) of Fairies, where women of all shapes, sizes and origins were trained in dance, drama and music. Needless to say, the king also enjoyed carnal relations with most, if not all the *paris* (fairies). The complex had gardens, open air theatres, gazebos, pavilions and fountains - all designed to pleasure the senses, and enable the artists to perform from time to time. The British were *persona non-grata* within the complex, although common citizens of Lucknow could have a glimpse of the premises during the annual *Jogiya Mela*, in which the king himself participated with gusto. Wajid Ali's medieval mindset and social norms were anathema for the Victorian British, who labelled the king as a debauch and a wastrel. Lucknow in 1856 was a heady mix of power politics, greed, sex and indolence. The city and the kingdom of Awadh as a whole were heading for a horrific tragedy with single-minded determination.

Radha looked around the room given to her by her father with some trepidation. It was cavernous by any standards, but forlorn. All royal accoutrements had been stripped off long ago, making the place gloomy, where one's voice echoed and the clattering of footsteps was evident, in the absence of carpets. Her family had left their ancestral estate, with its mud fort and moat lined with thorny bushes - preferring to make Lucknow their new home, under the patronage of the British. An army of servants were moving around from room to room, gauging the requirements, which would provide

Fig. 1: Vintage photograph of erstwhile *Pari Khana*, Kaiserbagh, Unidentified Photographer.

a semblance of comfort to the family and its retinue of serfs. It was immediately obvious that the *kothi* would need extensive repairs, followed by furnishing afresh. But it was a tall claim. Lucknow city was in shambles, with masons and artisans nowhere to be found and suppliers of creature comforts non-existent.

That night, unable to sleep, Radha looked out from her window. It was around midnight, but the new place made her sleepless. The young princess had no siblings to talk to, her elderly parents were long asleep and the huge retinue of servants and attendants almost comatose with fatigue. At this unearthly hour, Kaiserbagh looked almost surreal. The Safed Baradari or *Qasr-ul-Aza* in the middle of the garden complex shone in the reflected light of the moon. The horrors that Kaiserbagh had faced in 1858 were not obvious at least now - the silence all around was soothing. From the distance, Radha saw a lone horseman slowly entering the gardens through the western *Lakhi Darwaza*. The sound of hoofs was muffled, the horseman bore no arms, but at close quarters, he seemed to be bearing a sheaf of roses. The horse silently clomped towards the *Pari Khana* and seemed to vanish in the shadows. Radha felt a strange sort of empathy towards the stranger. Perhaps it was her loneliness that made her so. Her last thought, before she dozed off to a fitful sleep was that she could not see the horseman's face.

Radha spent much of her time decorating her new home, now rechristened as *Naraingarh House*, with particular focus on her own room, with whatever sparse furnishings and decorative elements that her father could manage to procure from the now ruined markets of Lucknow and nearby Cawnpore (Kanpur). Daytime was hot but as the sun went down, she took to exploring the area, sometimes accompanied by the children of other *ta'aluqdars*, who were in a similar plight. They marvelled at the enormous open air theatre called *Lanka*, now in ruins, the artificial pond with its marble bridge and the desolate *Pari Khana*, which had been left to quietly deteriorate - it had not been earmarked for any purpose by the British or their cohorts. Once, while standing before the desolate building where Wajid Ali Shah's "fairies" had cavorted not so long ago, Radha suddenly recollected that the lone horseman she had seen at midnight had apparently entered the portals of this very building, before vanishing in the gloom. Radha was not faint-hearted, but somehow, she could not find courage to enter the building which seemed strangely forbidding and dismal in the twilight. A strange sexual tension enveloped her when she had been taking stock of this immense building from outside. She could not understand the restlessness within herself, and neither was anyone there to narrate to her about the *Pari Khana* and its lurid history. Radha retraced her steps and hurriedly walked towards her new home, her heart fluttering and mouth dry, resolving never to go near the *Pari Khana* again.

Time flew by, and within a year, most of the *ta'aluqdars* and their families had settled in the various *kothis* (mansions) allotted to them in Kaiserbagh. Many allottees had carried out the necessary repairs and surreptitious internal modifications, which were understandable. In the meantime, the colonial rulers had remained busy in the landscaping of Lucknow, as per British norms. This was achieved by mercilessly demolishing buildings and cutting straight roads across the city. Kaiserbagh was no exception; many of its gateways, *baradaris*, pavilions and gazebos were removed and a new road, running through the premises bisected the palace-garden complex into roughly two equal parts. The *Safed Baradari* had been repaired, the height of its roof raised and the shattered domes on its four corners removed - future generations would not even know that gilded domes had ever existed atop this place of mourning, now modified for hosting cultural get-togethers and official programs. The building of the erstwhile *Pari Khana* continued to stand, its condition now even more gloomy and forbidding. Often Radha would observe the structure from her window, but could never gather the courage to enter the premises even in the day time.

It was a hot summer night, and there had been a social gathering of sorts in the newly landscaped garden of *Kaiserbagh*, with Lucknow's neo nobility and a few British officials gathering for drinks and dinner. After returning to her room, Radha could not sleep. Close to midnight, she decided to stop tossing and turning in her bed and instead, breathe in the fresh air from her window. But what she beheld turned her blood to ice. The same faceless horseman she had seen earlier was cantering noiselessly across the garden premises, but this time, he was carrying a sword. Man and horse raced at full speed towards the *Pari Khana*, where a woman in a *hijab* (veil) ran out to meet him. He pulled the woman up on his horse, but by this time, there was a commotion and a dozen or so Nawabi style soldiers appeared, swords and daggers in hand. The lone horseman headed towards the eastern gate, brandishing his sword, but was cut down by the soldiers and pulled down from the horse. The woman also fell to the ground and was dragged away within the *Pari Khana* building. All this happened within a matter of seconds before Radha's astonished eyes. The scene then cleared and everything was as desolate before. Silent, and almost petrifying in its stillness.

Radha collapsed on her bed, her heart beating wildly. In her terror, she felt nauseated and almost gagged, throwing up the evening's dinner on the floor. From childhood, she had seen many blood thirsty scenes in the rustic fort where she had been born and gained adolescence. Being a single child, she was gutsy and fearless. But that was the normal physical world. What she had perceived just now was something supernatural. She had no one to turn to, no one to discuss her fears and apprehensions with - her father being the typical rural overlord and mother being the quintessential gossipy type, more interested in clothes, jewellery and ladies' banter. After her breathing had stabilised and heartbeat returned to normal, she lay back, closing her eyes and trying to recollect as to what she had just seen and its possible rational explanation. But rationality escaped her. She fell into a disturbed slumber, and only woke up the next day with a splitting headache. Otherwise, everything was normal as usual.

The idea of setting up a training school for women having an aptitude for singing, dancing and even dramatics had the brainchild of a youthful Wajid Ali Shah, during his days as a prince and heir-designate to the Awadh throne. His father, Amjad Ali Shah, the reigning king, looked down upon his son's activities with disapproval, but as expected, could not curb him - having repudiated Mustafa Ali, Wajid Ali's elder brother earlier. A "house" later known as *Rashq-e-Iram*, was set aside by Wajid Ali for training nubile young women in song and dance. This house would later metamorphose into the full fledged *Pari Khana* after Wajid Ali took over the reigns of Awadh in 1847 and the Kaiserbagh palace complex was speedily built in his typical expansive style. For quite sometime, a certain Najm un-Nisa Begum remained on security detail at *Pari Khana*. After her demise, the charge was given to an Umrao Begum, on the recommendation of *daroga* Mohammad Hussain Ali Khan, who was in charge of the palace security as a whole. Umrao Begum did not prove to be as efficient as Najm un-Nisan, and the frequent indiscretions of the *paris* remained unnoticed and unreported. Wajid Ali, although having the countenance of a benevolent ruler, could be ruthless at times, including his punishment and banishment of *paris* who crossed the line. The *paris* too lost no opportunity in exerting their hold over the young king, by fair means or foul, which rankled the ruler and caused him much angst. Moreover, the *paris*, many of whom were of doubtful virtue, did not hesitate in surreptitious sexual escapades, despite the risk involved.

Shaukat was the youthful son of *daroga* Hussain Ali Khan, who had been recently inducted in the *Tircha* cavalry regiment of the king. The handsome youth was an expert swordsman and skilled horse rider. His father being the *daroga* of *Kaiserbagh* afforded him the privilege of moving around unhindered within the palace complex on horseback, while the *paris* milling around cast appreciative glances at him. Not that Shaukat showed any interest, but once his glance fell on Mumtaz and it was love at first sight. Although a mere soldier, his physical attributes and personality far exceeded the king's countenance, which was portly, the king himself being prone to erratic outbursts. Naturally, any rendezvous in daytime was out of question, but Shaukat found a way out. He persuaded his father to assign him on night patrol duty, which the ageing *daroga* agreed to, oblivious of his son's intentions. In dark nights, his movements were shielded and his passionate trysts with Mumtaz near the *Pari Khana* went unnoticed for sometime. But on moonlit nights, it was clear that instead of carrying his sword, Shaukat often carried a bunch of flowers, typically red roses for his beloved. As in most love stories, the time was ripe for confrontation and tragedy.

Fig 2: Shaving the head of a *Pari* as punishment, *Ishqnama* (1849), Wajid Ali Shah

Mumtaz came to know from other *paris* who were sympathetic to her cause that the details of her affair had reached the ears of the king, and swift, merciless retribution was soon to follow. She then decided to elope with Shaukat the very next day, to which her lover agreed. The young soldier entered the palace complex as usual, but unfortunately, it was the night of the full moon. Knowing the inherent danger, he drew his sword and galloped at full sway towards the *Pari Khana*, where his beloved awaited him. They had planned to ride all night on horseback and leave the city of Lucknow far behind, moving by nights and hiding in daytime, till they had left Awadh and crossed over into British territory of Allahabad. But on that night, fate had other plans. The king's soldiers from the rival *Banka* regiment gave chase and pulled him down from his horse. One slash of a sword severed Shaukat's head from his body. Female guards then rushed out from within the *Pari Khana*, grabbed Mumtaz and dragged her inside. Shaukat's body and head were hurriedly wrapped in gunny bags, and two cavalry soldiers rode all night till they reached the outskirts of Sitapur, where they threw their burden into a marsh. It was imperative that *daroga* Hussain Ali Khan should not know what had happened to his son. That fateful moonlit night did not bring roses for the unfortunate Mumtaz - it brought death and grief for the girl who had been hankering for her lover and had planned a future together with him.

The next day, a furious Wajid Ali ordered that Mumtaz be banished from Lucknow, but not before she had been soundly whipped, her back torn to shreds. But when Mumtaz, weeping and shackled, was brought in Wajid Ali's presence, the youthful ruler calmed down, recollecting that other *paris* had done much worse, but had gotten off with lighter sentences. Despite being a ruler with a medieval lineage, Wajid Ali was neither blood-thirsty, nor did he believe in unnecessary barbarism. The young king also remembered the intimate moments that he had shared with her, and his heart relented. Instead, he ordered that Mumtaz be tied to a tree and her hair to be shorn off, before being banished from *Pari Khana*. She would be free to remain in Lucknow, if she so desired. But death was stalking Mumtaz just as it had been stalking her lover only a few hours ago. Ostracised from the court, her shaven head screened from public gaze with the help of a *dupatta*, as the sobbing, penniless girl entered Golaganj, hoping to seek shelter with some of her relatives; a rampaging elephant appeared all of a sudden from nowhere. Passers-by, who panicked and ran helter-skelter, were trampled to death under its immense feet. Mumtaz was one of them.

It took Radha a long time to piece together, the various bits and pieces of this tragic story. It was generally accepted that Kaiserbagh was an eerie place, possibly haunted by restless spirits, but these were related more to the tragic battles and deaths that had occurred here and not due any love story. Aadil, an ancient, bent old man, pottering about in the garden of Radha's *kothi* proved to be a mine of information (and gossip) about Kaiserbagh. He claimed to have been in the service of the Nawabi elites, from the times of Nasir-ud-Din Haider. He had seen Wajid Ali's court and the life within, with his own eyes. The reason why the story about Shaukat and Mumtaz remained relatively untold was that Hussain Ali Khan was a man with powerful connections and all effort had been made to hide the truth about his son from reaching him. Aadil also claimed to have spoken to some of the *paris* in this regard, his old age giving him licence to move about where males were not allowed. As all gardens, the greenery around *Pari Khana* also needed tending. And there were no female gardeners. Hence the acceptance of Aadil in the premises was unhindered. He had met people, heard stories and seen incidents which could become the subject matter for a book in itself. The tragic story of Shaukat and Mumtaz was just one such story.

Strangely, after hearing the background story of this spectre horseman and his lover, Radha lost her fear for the gloomy ruins of *Pari Khana*. Somehow, it had reached out to her, giving her empathy for the women who had lived and died within the premises, whose trials and tribulations gave the place a unique aura, which everyone could not sense.

Nevertheless, from that day onwards, Radha resolved not to gaze anymore at the ruins from her window on moonlit nights.

ӁӁӁ

The Cursed Gateway...
Phansi Darwaza

"When suspected rebels were given the courtesy of a trial, although they were invariably found guilty, hanging was frequently used, either from trees or from sturdy wooden gallows erected at strategic places. There was a particular emphasis on the symbolic placing of the gallows - it had to be at a public site, but it also had to be a site of significance for the rebels. At Lucknow, four gallows were built in the gardens of the Qaisarbagh Palace... another was erected on the lawn behind Barowen, at Musa Bagh..."

-Rosie Llewellyn Jones, Historian

Kulvinder Singh, aged about 7 years, had always been a precocious child. He had accompanied his family migrating from Lahore to Lucknow after the Partition of 1947. He vaguely remembered the horrors, the screams, dying people and the destruction of buildings, including the rambling house where his family had resided. His father, Dalwinder, had lived with his extended family in the heart of Lahore, having several business interests, ranging from spices to silks. The family, like the others, had never anticipated that one day, they would be uprooted and lose everything they owned, getting the tag of "refugee" in newly independent India. From a happy, carefree existence, Kulvinder's childhood was now about to assume a tragic aspect.

Vast tracts of land in cities such as Delhi and Lucknow had become overrun by these unfortunate, homeless people from Pakistan, who were now without a roof over their heads. In Delhi, the tomb of Humayun and its grounds became an immediate shelter; in Lucknow it was Alambagh, then on the outskirts of the city, on the road between Kanpur and Lucknow. Alambagh was an extensive, fortified palace-cum-garden complex, enclosed by buttressed walls, nine feet high, having bastions at the four corners. A British plan of the premises indicated that the area of the garden complex was 1,440,000 square feet or about 33 acres. The palace itself was right at the centre of the garden with a single entrance through an impressive European-style gateway, bearing the usual fish symbol on its spandrels. Originally, the gateway to Alambagh was a squat, two storied structure, topped with triangular pediments on its north and south elevations. The entrance was composed of double archways, the outer ones being the usual cuspate ones, and the inner ones being plane. The archway spanned two storeys, and was flanked by two heterogeneous bays on each side, and the fish symbol in bas-relief on its spandrels. The tympanum of the pediment was pierced with a circular decorative opening, with the cornice sprouting leafy stucco projections and tiny finials. The palace complex was named after Alam Ara Begum, the *Khas Mahal* (chief consort / senior-most Queen and mother of the

Fig. 3: Ruins of Alambagh Gateway (1858), OM Lanyon.

crown prince or heir-apparent) of Wajid Ali Shah, who preferred to reside in her own palace, away from her husband, the king.

Alambagh was the scene was much action during the events of 1857 – 58. It was a stronghold of the Indian freedom fighters as a result of which the British relieving force, led by Colin Campbell, had to assault the building and secure it on November 14, 1857. Outram did not occupy Alambagh with his main force. Holding it with a small detachment and a few guns, he pitched his camp in the open, about a kilometre away. After wresting control of the premises, the camped British forces faced continuous assaults from Indian freedom fighters. Casualties were many and no prisoners were taken. It had been the unwritten rule during 1857 that no quarter would be asked for and no quarter would be given. Much before the temporary gallows were built in Kaiserbagh and Musa Bagh, the gateway of Alambagh became a place for quick hanging of Indian prisoners, without discrimination. Perhaps it was better than being mercilessly blown from cannons which was happening in nearby Bashiratganj and Mangalwar. Understandably the gateway acquired a notorious reputation and unfortunate sobriquet of *Phansi Darwaza* or Gateway of Hanging. Henry Havelock also breathed his last in Alambagh (he died of dysentery), on November 24, 1857, and was later buried near Alambagh Kothi. After the recapture of Lucknow, many Nawabi buildings were repaired and restored as per the requirements of the British, but Alambagh Kothi and the now infamous gateway were abandoned, being left to the mercy of nature.

After 1947, as refugee Sikh families continued to swarm in the area, the walls and the battlements of Alambagh were removed; only the ruined *kothi* and the now ominous looking gateway, broken in places and overrun by vegetation survived. The gateway no longer served as an entry point to the premises, the boundary walls was now gone. But the innocent Kulvinder was made of sterner stuff. All day he would roam around the refugee camp, moving to and fro from under the gateway without any restriction. But one day, he complained to his mother about feeling feverish, who promptly made him lie on the camp bed to sleep if possible - in any case, neither any doctor nor medical facilities were at hand. In the evening, Dalwinder entered the camp and came to know about his young son's ailment. He found Kulvinder sleeping deeply, but as he put his hand on his sleeping son's shoulder, the little boy awoke with a jerk. His eyes were rolled back and he started muttering gibberish in a hoarse, manly voice. Dalwinder felt a chill up his spine, but he patted his son's shoulder and somehow made him lie on the camp bed once again. The child fell asleep promptly, but tossed and turned all night, muttering in his sleep, watched over by his worried, tearful mother.

The next day, Kulvinder was his usual self, and the family was relieved, attributing the child's strange behaviour being due to high fever. Although his mother forbade him to move out, the child that he was, Kulvinder played his usual games with his siblings and friends. It was during an innocent game of hide and seek that the child sneaked off in search of a suitable hiding place, and what could be better than the abandoned gateway, where no one ever went? As hours passed by, search parties were now organised to find the child. Finally as evening was approaching, a posse of Sikh youth found Kulvinder in one corner of the gateway, curled up on the floor, in a semi-conscious state. As they made to lift him, the child abruptly sprang up and flung a volley of abuses at his rescuers. The most appalling part of this episode was that now Kulvinder spoke in a harsh man's voice, in broken *Farsi* (Persian), intermixed with rustic Hindustani. His eyes blazing with an inner fire, he stood erect, chest heaving proudly. The migrant Sikh youth were not familiar with the language of Awadh - they could not make head or tail of what Kulvinder was ranting about. But the bellowing, aggressive tone from the child chilled their hearts. Grabbing the now struggling child by his arms, legs and waist, they half carried, half dragged him to his parents' camp, depositing him on the camp bed with a thump. As the appalled family watched, Kulvinder heaved and jerked then collapsed in a comatose state. The night passed, with the terrified parents and other well-wishers crowding around the camp and speaking among themselves in whispers. A horror had come to visit them in this camp - a horror more horrifying than what they had recently experienced during the riots. Because this time, no human's hand was at work - some supernatural evil was abroad.

It was during the routine hangings of Indian prisoners by General Outram and his fellow officers that a firebrand leader from the area, Bandé Hasan, popularly known as Banké Bihari, due to his devotion for Lord Krishna, had been captured and sentenced to hang, without any statutory trial. Banké was a one-man revolutionary - he reported to no command. He specialised in reconnoitring missions and guerrilla tactics. Once he was convinced of a security gap in the enemy's camp, he would creep inside, taking advantage of their vulnerability during dawn, and manage to throttle one or two soldiers from the enemy side. This continuous stream of murderous deaths of his soldiers confounded Outram, who had camped beyond the Alambagh grounds and was exposed to the countryside from all sides. It was impossible to secure the entire area and as the early morning assaults raised the death toll, the wily Outram decided to put horses on guard duty, which would whinny on seeing any approaching stranger. In one such foray, as Banké approached the camp, an alert horse whinnied and clomped his hoofs on seeing the stranger. The alerted British solders on guard duty fell upon the intruder and put him in irons within no time at all. In day time, as Outram pronounced the death sentence, the proud Banké, his chest heaving with pride, asked that he be hanged without being blindfolded or hands tied - he wanted to survey his beloved motherland for the last time, before he died. The General had no time for sentimentalities - he ignored Banké's last request, had him trussed up and led to the gallows. It was at this point of time that the firebrand Indian revolutionary let loose a volley of abuses and threats to the British, uttering a curse that the British would not find a moment of peace after his death and they would be forced to quit his beloved country in the years to come.

Banké was hanged without further ado, his still twitching body thrown in a nearby *nullah* or drain and covered lightly with soil, like other prisoners executed earlier. Incidentally this was the last hanging at Alambagh Gate, and curses apart, the British would be constrained to abandon the outpost due to a variety of reasons.

It now appeared that the disincarnate, vengeful spirit of Banké had roamed the premises of Alambagh for decades and had now inexplicably possessed the body of a young innocent child.

Apparently, the laws of the spirit world are different from that of the corporeal world, where logic and ethics of the living do not count. The desperate family consulted several holy men of different faiths in an effort to exorcise the vengeful spirit in control of Kulvinder, but in vain. Although the feral outbreaks lessened, the child grew listless and anaemic within a few months. In abject poverty, and in the absence of either medical advice or support otherwise, confined to a completely new place, far from their home at Lahore, Kulvinder breathed his last in the arms of his sobbing mother and shocked father.

Later, it would be known that Kulvinder had died on the very day that Banké had been hanged by the British General, 90 years ago.

ЖЖЖ

The Portrait

George Duncan Beechey belonged to a family of portrait artists; born in 1798 in London, he arrived in India in 1828 and took up the assignment as court painter during the reign of Nasir-ud-Din Haider and remained so in the court of Awadh, till the death of Mohammad Ali Shah in 1842. Apparently, he married a princess from the royal family, which gave him access to the royal court, facilitating his painting of portraits for royalty. Beechey died in Lucknow in 1852 and was buried in the Madiaon cemetery of Lucknow. It is said that his demise was due to grief, because the ship carrying his best portraits to England for exhibition, had sunk in the sea, before reaching their destination. For this very reason, his artworks are very rare to find and also very expensive. Beechey's restless spirit reportedly continued to his former house in Madiaon Cantonment of Lucknow, which was later occupied by Rev. Polehampton, Chaplain of Lucknow.

Portraits are meant to be displayed, not stored in dusty storerooms, hidden away from public eye. In the days of yore, when photography was not available, portrait artists were very much in demand. These artists would produce great works of art for their patrons, using a variety of media, including oils, charcoal, pencils and tempera (pigments dispersed egg yolk). These painters were paid fabulous sums for their works of art, many of which can now be seen in museums and heritage homes today. One such vivid oil colour painting depicting a regally dressed, voluptuous young woman and tentatively called *The Begum* turned up in art circles of Lucknow after the events of 1857. It was definitely a Nawabi era painting, fortunately remaining intact despite the frenzied looting and killing by British and Sikh soldiers after the British regained control of the city under Colin Campbell. The portrait was a large 48"x 36" creation with an ornate gild frame, which made it look even larger. During the frantic search for valuables, it appeared that a marauding British soldier had come across the painting lying in one corner of one of the lesser used rooms of the Chattar Manzil palace. Covered with dust and cobwebs, it did not seem too valuable. In any case, it was too large and heavy to be spirited away and sold off for a pittance. The painting continued to lie neglected, although in due course of time, word of its existence reached the ears of a certain Captain Ellis, of the Royal Engineers.

Later on, the victorious British converted the Chattar Manzil palace to the United Service Club, while a portion of the neighbouring Farhat Baksh palace would be provided to the Union Club for the less elite uncovenanted, petty officials of British officialdom. It was during the renovation and repair work of the Chattar Manzil, this time under British supervision, that the workmen and masons came across this neglected painting once again. When the news

Fig. 4: Chattar Manzil Palace as United Services Club (1880), Unidentified Photographer.

reached by word of mouth to the same Captain Ellis, who by now was supervising the renovation work, he was reminded of the news that he had received earlier through a petty sergeant during the loot of the Nawabi properties, then under Campbell's implicit consent. Ellis hurried to the site, and finding the painting in reasonably good condition, ordered that it be hung in the main dining hall of the palace. Strangely, it proved to be easier said than done. The painting was abnormally heavy, suggesting the use of heavy oil impasto by the unidentified artist; it required three workmen, who lifted it gingerly, dusted it clean and proceeded to the second storey of the palace, where Ellis wanted the painting to be installed at a vantage point. Unfortunately, while climbing the steep stairway in comparative darkness, one of the workmen missed his step. The result was that the weight of the painting fell on the other two, who could not bear the sudden load; all three came crashing down, together with the painting. The latter did not seem to suffer much damage but one of the workmen suffered severe head injuries, which proved to be fatal. He was dead by evening.

Ellis took the accident in his stride. After all, the workmen were Indian natives and wholly expendable. The shifting work was continued the next day, this time with the help of five workmen. The portrait was installed at a vantage point, overlooking the length of the dining hall. The unknown *begum* would gaze down with regal authority at the British officials and their spouses, who would soon relish their luncheons and dinners at the majestic dining table from the Nawabi era.

The flurry of construction activity continued at a frenetic pace at the Chattar Manzil and neighbouring Farhat Baksh, as the colonial administration wanted to assume the use of these two palaces as soon as possible. Many officials, recently posted at Lucknow were without suitable accommodation, and it had been decided that quite a few could be accommodated in many of the commodious, if rather gloomy rooms of the palace complex - at least temporarily. The officials were clamouring for boarding and lodging and the Lucknow of that period was a city of ruins. There was hardly any building which did not bear the ravages of the bloody warfare that had laid the city waste just a few months ago. However, despite the frenetic pace of reconstruction, it took a full year to make the environs of Chattar Manzil liveable. But not before another tragedy occurred in the palace, which, this time, alerted the colonial administration that all was not well with the premises, which they had selected as one of many, due to its imposing appearance and vantage location. The palace had underground passages, which were connected to other buildings in the vicinity. Access to the passages were dark and intimidating, as blind turns veered off, leading to nowhere, while other paths led to dark basement rooms or *tykhanas.* A posse of construction workers who were trying to navigate the passages in the dark, aided by hand-held lamps came across a room in one corner; the room was securely sealed with a substantial medieval era chain and bolt. On breaking open the entrance, the workers were stunned to find instruments of torture in the room lying haphazardly. But what chilled them was the presence of two skeletons, shackled to the walls. The skeletons were mouldy and the torture instruments like pincers and thumbscrews, lying on a makeshift wooden table were ancient and rusted. It was obvious that the room had been sealed long ago and forgotten, together with the humans inside, whoever they were.

The terrified workmen retraced their steps hurriedly and stumbled up the stairs, where they related their experience to others in their group. Having decided not to go near the dungeon room henceforth, they resumed work in other areas of the massive palace complex. Among the workmen was a wizened old man, with dull rheumy eyes and a stooped posture. He was respectfully called *chacha jaan* (uncle) by others, although his real name was Bilal. Despite his age and frail appearance, he was a capable worker, who never shirked from his duties like some of the youngsters around him. In fact, he was a favourite of the labour contractor, who was supervising the renovation work. Bilal had been working in the area for the last several decades, firstly in the Nawabi court and now under the British masters. The story of the hidden dungeon left him unmoved. He had heard about it when he was a youth and the Nawabi rule was at its zenith. Presently, he had been assigned to clean and polish the dining hall of the palace to make it suitable for use. The old man, holding his mops, rags and cleaning liquids shuffled to the hall and started to work in right earnest. The hall was dimly lit, even in daytime, and as he rubbed and polished the massive dining table, his eyes fell upon the recently installed portrait of the unknown *begum* on the wall in the far corner of the hall. At first he couldn't believe what he saw. Shuffling closer and rubbing his eyes, he gazed at the portrait; even in the semi-darkness, the portrait appeared to be eerily luminescent and it seemed to him that the *begum* was looking straight into his eyes with a malicious, malevolent look. As long forgotten memories crowded his mind, Bilal gave a yell and made as if to flee from the hall. But his feet felt leaden. His mind was swamped by a turmoil of emotions and his frail body trembled like a leaf in the wind.

Bilal's compatriots found him much later, when they were winding up the days work and preparing to leave. The old man was stone cold dead, his eyes wide open and tongue protruding from his mouth. It was obvious that his heart had given up, after encountering some unspeakable horror. No one would ever know what Bilal's last thoughts had been before he had died. Actually, he had recognised the woman in the portrait. She had been a maidservant in the harem of Nasir-ud-Din Haider, and a cynosure of all eyes, including Bilal himself, who was then in his youth. The licentious second king of Awadh, who had the habit of selecting female consorts at random, had tried to seduce Madiha (literally meaning a woman of praise) as well, due to her extreme beauty and perfect physical proportions. But Madiha had not yielded. She was already in a relationship with a young Turkic horse rider, Adeel and two had planned to marry soon and raise a family.

The king implored and coaxed her, assuring that he would elevate her to an even greater rank than that of Dulari or Mallika Zamani, the so-called current favourite in the court. The king, by now, was tired of Dulari's constant demands for money and her insistence that Kaiwan Jah, her son from a former elephant driver, be declared as the legal successor to the Awadh throne. But Madiha was adamant in her refusal to bow down before the king's lecherous advances and the king was equally unrelenting in his desire to possess her. One day, he called Madiha to his royal chambers, but he was not alone. The court painter, George Beechey was seated near to the ruler, ready with his easel and equipage for painting. The king ordered the painter to create a portrait of Madiha, then and there, which he intended to install in his boudoir. But this was easier said than done. The entire exercise took about a month, during which Madiha would be obliged to strike a pose for Beechey in the anteroom and the king was gaze at Madiha's beauty, through long hours, to his heart's content. When the painting was complete, it was a stunning creation, with the girl appearing almost alive in the work of art. The king bade Madiha to approach him and made as if to embrace her, while showing her the portrait for the first time. The girl, dazed by the intricate details of her own portrait, was oblivious that the king had his arm around her waist and was gently caressing her breast. Upon the sudden realisation of the king's true intentions, she recoiled with a gasp, forcefully pushing him away, causing him to lose his balance and tumble onto his own bed. Beechey had already left the anteroom and Madiha was like a fawn before a ferocious tiger. But Nasir was strangely silent. He gestured to Madiha to leave the room and called out for his Chief of Guards. Within a short time, Adeel was arrested and thrown into the small dungeon of the Chattar Manzil, hands and legs in shackles. Madiha was dragged to the king's presence, the latter being silent but seething with anger. After taking a last look at her, he ordered that the girl too should join her paramour in the dungeon; however, he was unable to pronounce any harsh sentence against her. The dungeon was to be sealed off. Adeel and Madiha would never see the light of day again and death would visit them due to starvation and suffocation. The intricately painted portrait was to be taken away from the king's sight and thrown into the rubbish heap.

Thus, concluded the back-story of *The Begum*; however, the portrait in question depicted not a *begum* (woman of noble descent), but rather a female attendant from the Nawabi court. Despite the neglect, the painting managed to survive, but tragedy and misfortune accompanied it, wherever it was installed. In fact, the accursed painting was to soon claim its next victim, Captain Ellis, when it suddenly came loose and crashed down upon him, while he was gazing at it and wondering about its past and rather perplexing origins.

The British Isles have always been famous for hauntings and the British were no strangers to supernatural phenomena. Without further ado, it was mutually decided by the Club Secretary and Commanding Officer to discreetly remove the portrait from the dining hall and stack it with other unclassified artefacts collected from various sources. It was later moved to the Lal Baradari, where a Provincial Museum was set up in 1863, but the portrait was never put on public display. By 1883, after many vicissitudes, the Lucknow Museum got its own distinct identity (but not its own premises). *The Begum* continued to languish in storehouses and warehouses. It is believed that this forgotten painting, in all its glory, is still extant in the dark, dusty recesses of present day Lucknow Museum, away from public eye. But no one can vouch for this fact.

ЖЖЖ

The Lovelorn Ghost

Charles George Palmer, son of Lt. Colonel Henry Palmer of the 48th Native Infantry and a student of La Martiniere School (now College), Lucknow was merely nine years old when the rebellion or First War of Independence broke out in Lucknow in May 1857. At the Lucknow Residency, he was put on routine duties, together with other pupils, which included the grinding of corn, carrying ammunition and conveying messages. His 19 year old sister, Susanna arrived shortly from England. On July 1, she was mortally injured by a cannonball and had to undergo amputation of her leg. She could not survive the trauma and died on July 3, 1857. It is said that she was engaged to be married to an officer in the East India Company stationed at Lucknow. The identity of her supposed fiancé has not been established till date.

It had been a long and arduous journey for Susanna Palmer. To reduce her travel time, she had avoided the direct route to India by ship *via* the Cape of Good Hope on the tip of Africa, and preferred to board a ship from Southampton to reach Alexandria in Egypt; from there, she travelled by land across the Suez Peninsula to Port Suez on the Red Sea and then boarded another ship for Calcutta. Another seemingly endless journey by river boat and palanquins across the vast plains of northern India had finally ended at Lucknow. Although the searing hot summer took a toll of her health, Susanna, who seemed frail in appearance, appeared undaunted. Her father, Col. Henry Palmer of the 48th Native Infantry had taken away her mother, Susannah Elizabeth, Elizabeth Anne, her elder sister and Charles, her kid brother to India, leaving her behind in England, away from the grime and heat of India, to take care of her other siblings, Henry,

Mary, Anne and George. Her mother had died in 1856, before the outbreak of the rebellion. Elizabeth Anne was married to Lt. Ralph Ouseley, the Quartermaster of the 48th Regiment, NI and well settled in India. Now it was the turn of Susanna to get a suitable groom in Lucknow.

Col. Palmer had been leading a life of contentment in the Madiaon Cantonment at Lucknow, before the outbreak of the rebellion. But fate got him embroiled in a controversy and he would later be held responsible for the tragedy that occurred at Madiaon. The 7th Awadh Irregular Infantry stationed at Musa Bagh had refused to use the "greased" cartridges on May 3, 1857 and Henry Lawrence, Chief Commissioner, in a bid to spread the rebellion from spreading any further, decided to disarm them. The mutinous soldiers sent a letter to the 48th NI at Madiaon, seeking for help. This letter was intercepted by the Col. Palmer, then CO of Madiaon, who requisitioned European and Native Infantries from the city to proceed to Musa Bagh, thus leaving Madiaon wide open for the mayhem that was to follow. The

Fig. 5: Ruins of the Lucknow Residency (1890), Unidentified Photographer.

rebellion at Musa Bagh was quelled, but Palmer had underestimated the resentment among the native soldiers in his own camp, who finally broke out in rebellion on the night of May 30, 1857. The Indian rebels went on a rampage, killing their British officers and setting fire to all the 21 officers' bungalows in the cantonment. Palmer, who was lucky to get away with his life, was later given charge of the *Macchi Bhavan* fort, and then finally shifted to the Residency.

On her arrival, the unfortunate Susanna caught just one glimpse of her future husband, a Captain in the 42nd NI. Shells and cannon balls whizzing past every few minutes and sounds of explosions were not very conducive for a romantic tryst between the two. A small welcoming had been organised by Elizabeth Anne for her younger sister. The men, including Col. Palmer and Lt. Ouseley were obviously away, busy with their gruelling duty. A brief hello, a handshake and a cup of tea with stale biscuits were all that this unfortunate couple would ever have. The Captain rushed back to re-join his compatriots and a trembling Susanna collapsed on the settee, with Elizabeth Anne looking on sympathetically. In another

Fig. 6: Mural of Susanna Palmer, Lucknow Residency Museum (2023), Author.

two days, Susanna would die a horrible death, after getting her legs amputated through a botched up surgical operation by Dr Fayrer, the Residency surgeon. The unfortunate girl would not even get a grave or a tombstone of her own. Her body would be wrapped in sheets stained with blood from the amputation, and she would be interred under the cover of darkness in a designated area that served as a "community graveyard," despite the fact that her remains were not those of an anonymous, unrecognized person.

Following the British recapture of the city in 1858, a decision was taken by the colonial government to preserve the damaged structures of the Residency in their current state, together with meticulously tended gardens, which would serve as a memorial park. The premises were intended to honour the "victory" of the "gallant" British forces over the so-called "enemy." However, it should be recognized that in this particular context, the "gallant" were, in fact, the oppressors and invaders who had seized the lands of the indigenous people; the latter were now called the "enemy" merely for their efforts to reclaim their territories and dignity.

The Lucknow Residency premises was the site for an estimated 2000 deaths, due to various causes, including shelling, disease and epidemics like cholera. That its ruinous buildings, with their brooding appearance and former grandeur lying bare against the winds of change can still evoke a feeling of gloom and consternation in present times is well accepted. For example, an attendant in the premises for the past several decades, narrated that although the spirits could not be seen, muffled voices could be heard in the *tykhana* (basement which had housed the women and children of officers during the siege) from 11 pm till sunrise. It has been reported that employees (names withheld) working on the conservation and restoration of the area have also been victims of unexplainable phenomena. One employee even claimed that while surreptitiously attending to nature's call near the cemetery, his face was rubbed against a wall and later, he was thrown up and down on a *charpoy* (cot) in broad daylight. His condition worsened and ultimately the authorities had to transfer him to the Dilkusha Gardens. Another employee felt as if someone was pelting stones at him near the cemetery and he heard strange noises while returning home. This was felt by none, but was enough for him to change his route. Senior officials, on the other hand, deny all these tales of haunting, although they himself could not explain why an Exhibition at Aitkin's Guard was burnt down in a flash fire, without any identifiable cause. The wraith of a young girl clad in white and slowly moving from the doorway of the main building to the community graveyard (now provided with a protective iron grill and a commemorative plaque) has been reported by several visitors, who had the gumption to stay in the premises after twilight. The face of the wraith, though unclear, appears to be streaked with tears, as she slowly vanishes near the community graveyard. Some have claimed that she does not actually move, but hobbles, indicating the loss of her legs. Could this the restless, wandering spirit of the lovelorn Susanna Palmer, who was destined to die a horrible death in Lucknow, cutting short her youthful life, for no good reason than a senseless war between the marauding British and the defiant native population, who refused to take things lying down? The appearance of this tragic figure has been often reported on Friday nights; hapless Susanna had also died on a Friday a long time ago. Could there be a connection?

Due to the shortage of space, several people who died in the premises during the events of 1857 were often buried in layers, one on top of the other. These burials were carried out at night, accompanied by hurried prayers, since there was always the inherent danger of the occasional sniper shot from the sepoys stationed outside. It is conjectured by the locals that these restless spirits still wander in the premises after dusk, searching for food, or even for a proper place to rest. Many people claim that a couple of years ago, a headless Englishmen would roam around at night asking for a bottle of beer and a newspaper from people, which when given, he would walk away. On the other hand, there is a *mazar* (shrine over the grave of a holy man) of Sayyid Qasim Baba which even existed prior to the construction of the Residency. He is called "the pious one" and is occasionally seen by some under a banyan tree, clad in a white dress walking silently and ultimately vanishing. "Respect to the dead is of utmost importance and even accidental stepping on graves may cause serious harm to some," says an official rather sombrely. Interestingly, many of these spirits seemed to get satisfied when offered cigarettes and tea.

Most residents of Lucknow avoid the Residency premises after dark, even though the area is well-lighted and sound-and-light show is sometimes available after sunset for heritage buffs. Walking among the ruins of the St. Mary's Church and the desolate graves, one does experience an eerie sensation, almost as if an entire spirit world is co-exists side-by-side the mortal visitors; the only difference being that the spirits can silently observe the mortals, but the latter can only sense the presence of these restless spirits.

Post-script: The Ouseleys had two young sons, Ralph and Gore. The children fell ill and died within a few hours of each other on September 20, 1857. Their unfortunate mother, Elizabeth Anne, the elder sister of Susanna, aged 24 years, contracted dysentery and died of shock and dehydration on November 14, 1857. Their Epitaph reads, "The Lord gave and the Lord hath taken away. Blessed be the name of the Lord"

ЖЖЖ

Terror At Hewett Road

John Prescott Hewett served as Lieutenant Governor of the United Provinces of Agra and Oudh during 1907 - 1912. During the landscaping and laying of roads in colonial Lucknow, the road connecting Abbot Road (present day Vidhan Sabha Marg) to La Touche Road (present day Gautam Budh Marg) was named as Hewett Road (present day Shivaji Marg) in his honour. The Hewett Road area encompassed much of the former estate of Malka (or Mallika) Gheti, a junior (khurd) begum of Amjad Ali Shah, the second last king of Awadh and father of Wajid Ali Shah.

Post Independence, the area became a warren of homes and commercial establishments. However, if one looks around, remnants of Malka Gheti's properties can still be seen in the form of a dilapidated gateway, a karbala and old buildings constructed of lakhauri bricks from that era, in the compound popularly known as Ahata Rasool Beg. The begum was buried in an Imambara nearby, but neither her grave nor the Imambara can be discerned now due to heavy encroachments. A masjid, attributed to the begum is, however, is still extant in the area.

This story does not concern the properties of Malka Gheti, but a massive red coloured colonial-era building adjacent to *Malka Gheti Phatak* or gateway. Known to locals as *Lal Kothi*, the property still exists, but can no longer be observed from the road from any angle, as it is totally surrounded by concrete structures of all shapes and sizes, consisting of not only houses but also shops and showrooms, which have mushroomed all around the building. The entrance of the *Kothi*, with its typical portico, which squarely faced Hewett Road had a small open space - not exactly a lawn, but a vacant area which was encroached upon for a long time by the homeless and vagrants, together with the usual floating population of rickshaw pullers, *ekka-tonga* drivers and labourers. The portico cannot be distinguished now, being concealed behind a mass of unplanned shops and kiosks. Despite the prime location of the property and the massive premises of the building in question, no one has ever dared to enter it, claim it by legal or illegal means, or even damage it or occupy parts of it, which is a common enough occurrence in properties of similar nature across the city. So what is the mystery behind this? What has kept the land mafia away from claiming this as its own? Let us delve a little into the past and try to gather whatever little information is available which may be of interest to the reader.

Lucknow newspapers in the late seventies were suddenly splashed with details of the supernatural goings-on in the Hewett Road property. Apparently after lying vacant for several decades, a caretaker, named Harish had been appointed by the owners (who lived abroad). The caretaker shifted into the house with his small family and occupied two rooms for personal use, together with one small kitchen. It was a Herculean task to have the premises cleaned but the caretaker was undaunted. He set about his assignment, having decided to have the rooms cleaned one by one, instead of tackling the entire building at one go. Six labourers were appointed, together with two sweepers, the latter would clean the dirty washrooms and sooty kitchens to the extent possible. Painting and repair work would follow, if the owners agreed to bear the cost, which appeared to be doubtful.

The work commenced on a satisfactory note. The vagrants occupying the front porch left on their own, after seeing someone in authority inside the premises. The caretaker's family consisted of his wife and two young daughters, aged 5 and 7 years. They utilised one room as their bedroom and another as store-cum-general purpose room. They did not have the wherewithal to have a living room or dining room, but that was expected. One month and two went by and there was not an inkling of any problem. The labourers-cum-construction workers went about their daily routine of cleaning, repairing and of course, disposing the heaps of rubbish and debris, which had accumulated over the years in the un-occupied building. Things looked upbeat. But it would not last.

On an ordinary day, something extraordinary occurred. It was discovered that one of the labourers, Ramu, was not traceable, after lunch break. His absence was ignored for a while, but when he did not return by 5 pm, the matter was taken seriously by his co-workers, who reported his absence to the caretaker. In the swiftly descending twilight, and absence of electricity, a search was organised but it was futile. The quest for Ramu was abandoned at around 8 pm, the workers having decided to call it a day and return to their homes. Maybe Ramu had just walked off, due to some reason best known to him. Casual labourers shirking their duties and ceasing to work all of a sudden, to join some other labourer contractor was not a rare phenomenon. In fact, it was common enough in this line of work. Such workers mostly went about their duties as automatons. They had nothing to gain by being loyal, dedicated or faithful to the work at hand. Today it was some work, tomorrow it would be another. The lives of "daily wage" or "casual workers" or labourers followed this rootless existence. Ramu was just one such labourer.

After retiring to bed, with his family and enjoying a sound sleep for few hours, Harish, the caretaker awoke with a jerk. He felt that something was not quite right in the room, although his wife and children continued to sleep soundly. In the darkness, he thought he saw a shadow, which seemed to be beckoning to him. As his eyes grew used to the darkness, his blood chilled when he saw that it was Ramu, with blood streaming from his eyes, nose and mouth. The caretaker let loose a yell which made his wife sit up with a groan. After hurriedly lighting the oil lamp, both looked around to see if there had been anyone in the room. But it seemed to be Harish's imagination, playing tricks with his mind and eyes. Both husband and wife tried to sleep, this time with the oil lamp lit, which spread its feeble light across the room. But sleep eluded them that night, as it would elude them for many nights henceforth.

The next morning, Harish did not feel too well; he also did not see it proper to inform the other workers on the site about his nightmare.

Another emaciated labourer had already appeared before him, pleading for a chance to join the workforce as Ramu's replacement. Work had to be done; Harish capitulated and agreed to induct him in the team.

The nightmare was repeated on the second night and the next. Harish, who had started to sleep with a lit oil lamp decided on the third day to heed to the apparition's bidding and follow it to wherever it wanted Harish to accompany him. His heart thudding and brow sweating profusely, the caretaker walked with slow steps behind the apparition, which seemed to be gliding on the floor. The unnatural duo moved across the extensive premises, reached an outhouse and entered inside, where the apparition faded. In the semi-darkness, Harish thought he could see a well-like structure with an open mouth. Beside it, lying on the dusty floor was an iron grill, which seemed to have covered the well at some point of time but had now been shifted. Other than that, nothing was discernable. Harish retraced his steps but somehow his fear was gone. It was obvious that Ramu was now dead and the bloodied apparition, presumably Ramu's spirit, was trying to convey something; it meant no harm to Harish or anybody else. The caretaker decided to have the outhouse and the well explored thoroughly in the day time with his labour force. He slept peacefully that night.

At day time, an exploration of the outhouse revealed that the well was indeed a very dark, dank and deep structure, which had been covered by the rusted iron grill lying on one side. It appeared that Ramu had moved the grill and then vanished. But where was he? Had he fallen inside the well and died? Two daredevil workers volunteered to explore the depths of the well, after tying themselves securely with ropes and being lowered one by one into the depths, supported by others. As the first worker was thus lowered, his eyes adjusting to the gloom, his body brushing against the uneven surface of the side walls, he could see that the level of the water, dark and filthy, had receded far below and a number of objects were also floating inside. These included rusted swords, daggers and a helmet of sorts. As the rope lowered him further, he could make out a putrefying corpse floating in the dank water, its face slashed and bloodied, possibly as it had hit one or more of the rusted weapons as it had crashed down.

The lowered worker gave a jerk to the rope which was supporting him and indicated that he would go no further. Raising his voice, he asked his fellow worker to come down so the corpse could be retrieved. When the second worker reached the depths in a similar fashion, he was holding a hurricane lantern, which threw light all around. The slashed corpse was Ramu's but there were at least three dismembered skeletons lying in the muck. It was obvious that at some point of time, people had either fallen into the well, or more logically, had been killed and their bodies thrown inside the defunct well, which was then covered up by the iron grill.

To cut a long story short, Ramu's putrefying corpse and the remaining skeletal remains were brought up after a long and arduous exercise, this time, involving the local police. The affair of the skeletal remains continued to be an unsolved mystery although the unfortunate Ramu, who had no one to claim his body, was cremated by the authorities after conducting a post-mortem, which did not indicate any foul play.

The maintenance and repair work at the building remained suspended for a week. Ramu's untimely and unnatural death had been traumatic for the team of workmen as well as for Harish. But life had to go on. It is not known what had happened to the other skeletal remains. But somehow, after this occurrence, the house seemed to develop a malefic influence. The workers would complain that their work would be disturbed, their tools would be scattered about behind their backs. Harish took all this on his stride. But his complacency was disturbed one day in a very abrupt and fearsome manner. It was while he was taking his frugal afternoon meal with his wife that he happened to look inside his glass of water. But the water appeared cloudy, almost black. It was as if some creature was inside the glass because the water was swirling. Harish threw the glass away from him which hit the floor and shattered. The water which was splattered was absolutely normal. But the horror was just beginning. That very night, his sleeping children woke up in the middle of the night, screaming that someone was dragging them away from the bed. Harish and his wife could see no one. But their blood chilled when they saw that the bed sheets were indeed lying on the floor; a moment ago, the children had been sleeping cozily, covered with the sheets. As the children cowered on their shared bed, they seemed to be able to see something in the corner of the room, which seemed to terrify them. What added to the nameless horror was that the parents could not see what was menacing the children. Jumping up, they took the children in their arms, trying to comfort them. Slowly, the threat seemed to recede. The husband and wife duo decided to stay awake and keep a watch over the children while they slept, sacrificing their own sleep. The night dragged on interminably and as the light of dawn hit the window of the room, the couple collapsed in their bed, to catch with whatever little sleep was possible now.

This sequence of events continued for three nights, with the nameless entity or entities menacing the children and not the adults. On the fourth night the situation took a turn for the worse. Harish, who had been sleeping fitfully, noticed that the previously dark room where they were sleeping appeared to be brightly lit. He opened his eyes to notice that some of their household goods in the corner of the room were on fire. Strangely there was no heat or crackling sound, but the fire raged on. Harish jumped out of the bed with a shout, rushing outside to fetch a bucket of water for dousing the flames. In the commotion, his wife and children had woken up and were cowering in their beds as Harish managed to put out the mysterious fire with two buckets of water. There was no further sleep for anyone that night.

The next night proved that the entity or entities haunting the premises had gathered strength and was becoming more malevolent with time. Harish had decided to stay awake and keep a watch over his sleeping family for as long it was possible. But after midnight, he dozed off. It is not known when he awoke with a sudden premonition of horror, but he perceived that the bed on which her wife was sleeping was on fire. In fact, the bed sheets were burning, the flames now hungrily licking at his wife's bedclothes. Strangely, his wife continued to sleep peacefully through all this, since there was no heat or smell of burning. The children too were sleeping serenely in their corner, without an inkling of the evil that was now stalking them. A terrified Harish again rushed outside, bringing in buckets of water to douse the flames. As the cold water hit her, his wife woke up with a scream, but she did not suffer any burn injuries due to this cold fire from the spirit world. It was another sleepless night for the beleaguered family. They would spend one more night in the room, after which Harish would be forced to take a final call on the situation and how to tackle this nameless horror which was now seemed to be stalking him and his family.

On their last night in the house, the family did not have an inkling of what would happen; sleep being out of question, they talked in whispered tones, with two small oil lamps providing their feeble light from two corners of the room. Suddenly there was an ominous rumbling sound throughout the premises, as if a huge lot of furniture was being shifted or dragged on the floors, all at the same time. A sense of suffocation by the petrified humans was evident as they faced a shortage of breath and started gasping. Suddenly Harish and his wife were pulled out of their beds by invisible hands and flung with tremendous force across the room. They landed on the floor with a thud, his wife screaming uncontrollably and Harish being tongue-tied with horror. However, they did not appear to have suffered any injury due to this. Getting up and gathering the children in their arms, they rushed out of the entrance of the building to the porch. This would now become their home for a few more days.

The next day, the arriving workmen were astonished to see the caretaker and his wife, in a dishevelled state, sitting under the porch, while their children slept, curled in one corner. The terrified family now narrated their experiences of the past several days to the workmen, who were sympathetic and extended full cooperation to the husband and wife duo, in whatever way they could. It was decided that the house was certainly not safe for living but the porch with its open sides should be safer. The workmen hurriedly moved the couple's sparse furniture and personal belongings to the porch, and strung tarpaulin sheets all around, so as to provide an element of privacy for the beleaguered family. The day passed without any work being done. The story also leaked out, so now there were curious onlookers and passers-by who were moving down Hewett Road. It may be noted that in those days, half a century ago, there was hardly any motor traffic in the area. The onlookers were mostly pedestrians or cyclists, and a constant stream of gazing eyes added to the consternation of the already unfortunate family. Two of the workmen volunteered to sleep in the house that night and see for themselves what it was all about. Accordingly, before the sun had set, they had erected makeshift beds in the very room that had been previously occupied by Harish. The night was peaceful for them. Nothing harmed them or disturbed them, which, unfortunately, made them suspect about the sanity of the caretaker.

The next day, the local newspapers had a small article dedicated to this "haunted house" but it was not that effective so as to arouse the curiosity of the general public. However, that night, the two daredevil labourers again went to the room for a good night's sleep. Around 2 am, there was a thundering noise throughout the building (strangely, nothing could be heard outside) and as the two men tried to gather their wits about them, their beds caught fire. As the flames leapt up to the ceiling within seconds, and the terrified labourers prepared to jump out of their beds, they were pulled up by unseen hands and thrown across the room, their heads dashing against the walls. As expected, the men had no burn injuries but the beds and the sheets were gutted. The men rushed out and shouting on top of their voices, reached the porch, where Harish was sleeping peacefully with his family. The night had turned into a nightmare, with locals gathering within minutes and everyone gazing at awe and terror as the two labourers narrated their experience within the building.

The next day, journalists from two prominent newspapers of the city arrived at the haunted location to conduct interviews with Harish and his family, as well as the labourers. The reporters also scouted around the neighbourhood, posing inquiries in an effort to gather background information regarding the purported haunting. But no one volunteered anything. However, the following day, both newspapers carried huge headlines about that "Haunted House in Hewett Road" which was sensational enough to attract a huge crowd of people in the vicinity from morning till evening. Two young men, supposedly students in a nearby college volunteered to spend the night in the house, asked for permission from Harish, who was non-committal.

The youth, equipped with torches, a lamp, pillows, floor mats, drinking water and a pack of cards entered the premises and went up to the room for spending the night as decided. Nothing happened for a long time, as they chatted, played cards, sipped water and looked around, obviously seeing nothing. Then abruptly, the lamp went out and both the young men felt that someone had grabbed them by their throats and was squeezing mercilessly in a bid to strangle them. It happened within seconds and the boys were unable to react. But both later narrated the fact that the hands gripping them by their throats were *huge*, definitely not human hands. Possibly as large as a gorilla's, and thickly covered with coarse hair. Both struggled against their invisible monstrous attackers for perhaps only few seconds, which appeared like hours. And then, suddenly the pressure on their throats was gone. However, their collective sigh of relief was abruptly cut short as they saw that their floor mats and pillows had now caught fire. The young men had had enough; gathering their wits about them, without making any attempt to douse the fire, they rushed out of the building, shouting at the top of their voices. Their experiences would again feature in the city's newspapers, this time with a bigger and more detailed coverage.

Within a month, at least four different attempts were made by people of different backgrounds to spend the night in the house. These included a professional *tantrik* (black magician), two spiritualists, one priest and two students once again. All were chased out of the building at around 2 am; all had similar experiences to narrate - the flames without heat, the thundering noise, the attempts to choke them and of course, two of the curious visitors who were thrown across the room with a deadly force and aim.

Harish, who was never disturbed in his temporary abode in the porch of the building, finally informed his employers about his inability to continue with his assignment. Accompanied with his family, he left for an undisclosed destination. The labour force was naturally disbanded after all these occurrences and the restoration / repair work of the building came to a standstill. No background information could ever be gathered regarding the haunting phenomenon which made newspaper headlines for about a month or so, before fading into oblivion. However, few observations could be made from the occurrences, which deserve thought: Firstly, no one was ever *physically harmed* during the supernatural attacks, although there were physical attacks. Secondly, all those who had experienced the phenomenon reported that the *flames were without heat.* The flames leapt up but did not burn the humans, nor was there any heat. Thirdly, the unexplained supernatural entities *never followed* the humans as they fled outside. It was almost as if the entities wanted the humans to flee, to leave the premises, but not cause them harm. And last but not the least, the porch which, although part of the building, was unaffected. The entities remained *inside* the building and never created any disturbance outside.

The mystery of the Hewett Road haunting remains unsolved till date. Perhaps some tragedy or a series of tragedies had occurred inside the building, and the spirits had somehow remained trapped inside the abandoned well, where the bodies had been carelessly thrown in, together with the murder weapons. Once the skeletons were disturbed and removed, out came those restless spirits, who had been waiting in the space-time continuum of the spirit world. These entities wanted nothing more than to be left alone. And on seeing the living trespassing in their abode, they threw a scare into the humans, but never with an intention to cause any harm, physical or otherwise.

And so we must end this narrative with a question mark, till such time that some authentic information finally emerges and explains the haunting and "terror at Hewett Road."

ЖЖЖ

The Pit of Punishment

The "Nawabi" phase of Awadh (and Lucknow) commenced from 1722, with the advent of Sa'adat Khan Burhan-ul-Mulk and culminated with Wajid Ali Shah being deposed in 1856. The Nawabi rulers, although possessing a medieval lineage were not known for acts of cruelty or bigotry. Although deeply religious and belonging to the Shia faith, they followed a policy of religious inclusiveness, which brought them close to their Hindu subjects - the latter being in a majority. This was one of the reasons for the success of their rather indolent rule - they preferred to administer their territories through a combination of religious and cultural syncretism, with non-Muslims often occupying high posts in the administration. Of course, in matters of law and order, as well as occasional political upheavals, the Nawabs could be rather ruthless with criminals, as well as with political upstarts.

Lucknow in the late 1940s was markedly different from its present-day bustling *avatar*. The city primarily consisted of the historic old quarter in the west, a remnant of Nawabi rule, characterised by traditional run-down residences and an abundance of Islamic architectural landmarks. In the east was the cantonment area, a well-structured township established by the British, post-1857, for its military personnel. The Lucknow Improvement Trust, founded in the 1920s during colonial rule, had developed few planned residential and commercial zones in the town, which were both spacious and impressive. Narrow highways radiated from the city in multiple directions, leading to Kanpur, Sultanpur, Faizabad, Hardoi, Rae Bareilly and Sitapur. These roads were bordered by large trees, providing shade and refuge for weary travellers. During the day, these highways, originally referred to by the British as "high roads," experienced minimal traffic, mostly by way of bullock carts or ramshackle motor vehicles, and were completely deserted after sunset.

The year was 1949. India had become a not-so Independent country (in fact, it was a Dominion of the Commonwealth) in 1947. The vast administrative gap created due to the departing British had left the economy of the new born "country" in shambles. Once the initial euphoria and fervent zeal had dissipated, the ordinary citizen found himself in pursuit of a means to earn a living and sustain his existence, however meagre it might be. Ramakant, from a neighbouring village, had set up a small shack on Faizabad Road, about five miles from Kukrail, roughly near present day Chinhat, described in old British *Gazetteers* as a "village lying on the metalled road from Lucknow to Fyzabad, at a distance of about 6 miles from the former." The name *Chinhat* was possibly derived from the term, *Chana Haat* or *gram market,* which had flourished in the area from the times of Ghazi-ud-Din Haider, the first king of Awadh. Ramakant's family owned a measly plot of land nearby, which hardly yielded any agricultural income, be it from grain production or vegetable cultivation. Marginal farmers like Ramakant were forced to become seasonal labourers during lean seasons. Ramakant had chose an easier way out by setting up his shack, and providing watery tea and pitiable snacks to weary travellers. At least he was safe from the back-breaking labour which his compatriots were forced to undergo during the hot summer months. The weekly market or *haat* in the area was one consolation for the tea-seller, as locals flocked to the area on that day and his tea-shop became a focal point for their gathering over a cup of tea. After the day's proceeds were over, at sunset, he would trudge wearily along the highway for about two miles, before he reached his village. Ramakant religiously avoided the shortcut that traversed diagonally over the shrubs and brambles across a rolling landscape, which would have brought him to his village nearly a mile closer. The reader might wonder why. Not only Ramakant, but all the villagers of the area avoided the forested area along the highway. And the reason was not just the presence of brambles, nettles and occasional wildlife, but something different. In fact, the stretch was reputed to be "cursed" and no local person worth his salt would venture there in day time, what to talk of night time. Cursed yes, but no one knew the exact reason for the "curse" and what it was supposed to be. It was just a place which was to be avoided and this tradition had come down by word of mouth from their ancestors.

Regretfully, the northern or "Indo-Gangetic" plains of India, typically Uttar Pradesh, face challenging climatic conditions throughout the year. The summer months are characterised by intense heat for extended durations, while winters bring with them severe cold and persistent fog. The monsoon period, although brief, is marked by heavy rainfall that frequently leads to flash floods and significant destruction. In fact, the weather in Uttar Pradesh and its capital, Lucknow, remains agreeable for only about four months or even less in a calendar year.

It was a day in the month of June. The searingly hot, dusty wind (called *loo* in local parlance), which originated from the deserts of Rajasthan and swept across the northern plains all day long, blew steadily without break. Ramakant was well aware that indiscriminate exposure to *loo* could result in heatstroke and a quick death if one was not careful. He had had hardly any sales during the day, and it was only during the late evening, after sunset, when a trickle of customers, mostly labourers working in nearby areas, reached his shack, on bicycles or on foot, for a customary cup of tea, that too prepared in an indifferent manner, before wearily trudging towards their villages. Time passed very quickly and it was already 7 pm when the villagers had finally left. While putting out the fire and arranging his utensils and other nick-knacks, Ramakant noticed that at some point of time, a stray dog had apparently entered the shack from the rear, exposed end of the shack and had not only devoured his stock of boiled potatoes, it had also messed up and possibly urinated on the shelf where the utensils were stacked. This was a shock to Ramakant, who immediately started to clean the rack, washing the utensils one by one and rueing his fate. He regretted that he had not fixed some planks in the rear of the shack, unwittingly inviting this tragedy to happen. The loss of his meagre provisions was another blow.

By the time the damage had been controlled, it was already 9 pm, and it would take about an hour of wearisome walking along the lonely highway, now pitch dark, before he would reach his village home.

A troubling notion suddenly occurred to Ramakant, as he contemplated taking the "forbidden" shortcut to his village, dismissing the tales of curses and associated ghost stories as mere superstition. Having spent his entire life in the area and working from his shack for the past two years, he had never encountered any evidence of such a curse. With the lantern from his shack in one hand and a stick in the other, he felt confident that he could reach home swiftly without any hindrance. These thoughts swirled in Ramakant's fatigued mind as he promptly set off toward his village, the day's paltry earnings securely tucked away in a fold of his *dhoti*.

Surprisingly, the meandering path he took across the forest reached a large clearing, which was a kind of depression. Not exactly a pit but a hollowed-out area. Strangely, the entire area glowed eerily in the dark and his legs felt leaden as he proceeded further down the path. As Ramakant reached the hollow, he started shivering uncontrollably, apparently in the throes of a tropical fever. All at once he collapsed on the ground, his bodily strength completely gone now, as if a paralytic stroke had wracked through his body. Lying prostrate on the ground, he remained fully conscious of his senses, although his limbs now refused to function and his throat remained paralysed so he could not call out for help. Ramakant was now able to discern shadowy figures, some mounted on horses while others were on foot. The riders appeared to be equipped with swords and spears, whereas the individuals on foot seemed to be captives, their hands bound behind their backs. These unfortunate souls were being herded toward the depression, pushed along by the spectral horsemen who prodded them with their sharp weapons. However, the prisoners never reached the depression "alive," as their heads were abruptly severed by the sweeping sword blades; their lifeless bodies disappeared into the shallow abyss, their severed heads tumbling down alongside the bodies in a grotesque dance of death. Ramakant, witnessing this horrific *danse macabre* with a sense of disbelief, struggled to maintain his sanity. Amidst the ongoing spectral slaughter, he summoned an immense effort and, with great difficulty, regained his voice, calling out hoarsely as he attempted to flail his arms and call for help.

It appeared that a spectral horseman or soldier could hear his mortal cries, because it reigned in his horse and turned back to look at Ramakant, lying helplessly on the ground. In the darkness, although the figure of the horseman was shadowy, its eyes glowed with an inhuman blaze. The phantom soldier raised its sword and slashed at Ramakant's throat in a single sweep, severing his head from his body. Ramakant's final conscious thought, as his head tumbled down the slope, was the profound injustice of fate and his own tragic, meaningless end. And then his life was snuffed out like a candle in the dark.

The following day, at dawn, a search for the missing tea-seller was organised by the villagers. This was prompted by the desperate pleas of his wife and children to the village head, or *sarpanch*, for assistance. The benumbed villagers searched the tea stall and combed the surrounding area, yet no trace of the shopkeeper could be found. Eventually, a few brave young men volunteered to venture into the "forbidden" zone, clinging to the hope that Ramakant might be located there. Their determination proved successful when Ramakant's lifeless body was discovered near a hollowed depression. Although there were no indications of violence, the expression on the deceased's face was one of terror; his eyes wide open as if they had beheld an unspeakable horror before death. Ramakant's head remained attached to his body, but a conspicuous red scar was visible, deeply etched across throat, suggesting that he had been attacked with a sharp instrument at some point of time. His wife insisted that she had never observed this scar during his lifetime.

The inhabitants of the villages nearby would remain blissfully unaware that the sunken area had once served as a site for executions during the Nawabi era. In the dead of night, individuals deemed criminals and those sentenced to death were brought to this location and executed by beheading, leaving their remains to the elements. Over time, the site became regarded as "cursed," attributed to the restless spirits of those who had been denied proper funerary rites and ceremonies. Vegetation ceased to thrive in the hollow, and even local wildlife, sensing an unnatural presence, would avoid the vicinity while foraging. The barbaric act of beheading was eventually abolished by the British, who replaced it with another cruel method: summary hangings followed by indiscriminate burials. Lucknow's tryst with tragedy would continue for another century.

ЖЖЖ

An Encounter with A Riderless Horse

The Punjab Cavalry was raised in 1849 as a component of the Punjab Irregular Frontier Force, tasked with maintaining order along the Indo-Afghan border. Following its involvement in the events of 1857 in Delhi and Lucknow, the Unit transitioned into a regular cavalry unit, alongside the Punjab Frontier Force. It took part in the Second Afghan War from 1879 to 1880. Subsequent to the frontier operations conducted between 1894 and 1898, the Regiment did not return to the frontier area, and the Punjab Frontier Force was integrated into the Indian Army.

By March 11, 1858, James Outram had captured two bridges across the Gomti river near the Residency (Rennie's Iron Bridge and Asaf-ud-Daula's medieval *Shahi Pul* or Stone Bridge), although heavy artillery fire by the revolutionaries later forced him to abandon the Stone Bridge. Outram's position was unique; he had waived his rank in deference to Havelock's experience and achievements, being a mere "volunteer", and holding his earlier civilian post of Chief Commissioner of Oude, even though he remained in the thick of the battle.

During the so-called First Relief, one-third of Havelock's force had lain dead and wounded in and around Lucknow, including his own son and he himself became besieged inside the Residency. Hence Colin Campbell, the Commander-in-Chief was determined not to repeat the mistakes committed by his predecessors. During the Second Relief, advancing with great caution, Campbell managed to gain control of rebel strongholds like Dilkusha, Sikandar Bagh, Shah Najaf, Begum Kothi and finally Kaiserbagh. Before the final capture of Lucknow, Begum Hazrat Mahal and her forces had retreated from Kaiserbagh - abandoning one by one, their strongholds in the city, and spreading to the countryside to continue the freedom struggle. After the fire brand leader, Maulvi Ahmadullah "Danka Shah" fled from Lucknow, the city was declared to be "clear" by the British. The date was March 21, 1858. No doubt there had been grave (pun intended) mistakes and blunders on either side. The Begum and the Maulvi did not see eye-to-eye, leading to frequent skirmishes between the followers of the two leaders. While the revolutionaries had fortified the city from the west side, they had left the eastern flank wide open, which Campbell used for his advance. The freedom fighters were unable to woo Nepal's Jang Bahadur but for this, they can be excused; Jang Bahadur had no time for sentimentalities, being more interested in immediate plunder and long term political patronage of the British. But this did not prevent him from providing asylum to Begum Hazrat Mahal, in exchange for her jewels.

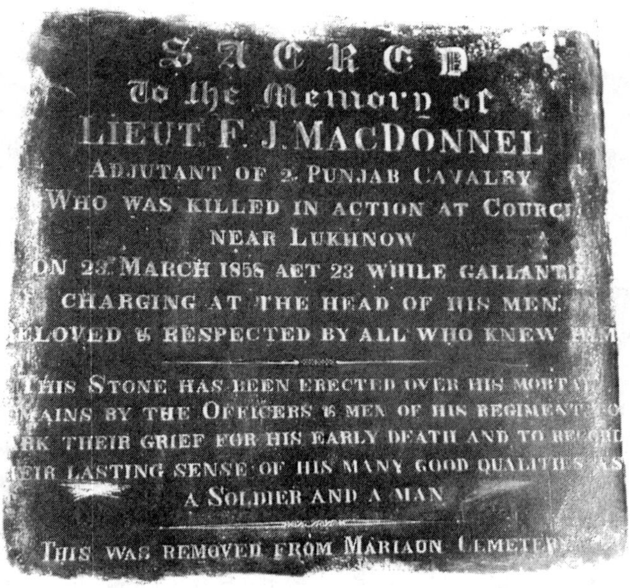

Fig. 7: Inscription on the grave of Lt. FJ MacDonnel (2023), Author.

On the British side, after their victory at Lucknow, a certain amount of complacency had crept in, coupled with fatigue. Indian freedom fighters had made good their escape from Musa Bagh, Kaiserbagh and other rebel strongholds, to the hinterlands of Awadh. Here, they were joined by the forces of the *ta'aluqdars* sympathetic to the cause of the Begum. But there was no unified command nor was there any strategic planning. Many of the British cavalry and infantry regiments, not directly involved in the action, perceived this to be the end of the bloody war, with soldiers and their officers eager to reach their respective camps, perhaps even reunite with their families, back in Lucknow and elsewhere. In this scenario, rode the men of the Punjab Cavalry on March 23, 1858, lead by Adjutant FJ MacDonnel, who had been on a routine reconnoitring mission from Daryabad (present day Bara Banki) to Lucknow *via* Courci (present day Kursi), then a small hamlet on the outskirts of Lucknow. Unlike what had occurred in the districts of Hardoi, Gonda and Lucknow, the whole body of *ta'aluqdars* in this area had joined the cause of the deposed king and revolutionaries. But they had offered no resistance at any moment, to the advance of British troops after the capture of Lucknow.

Lt. MacDonnel was a family man, who wished to re-unite with his young wife back at Lucknow as soon as possible; the young officer was also a keen admirer of the infamous Stephen Raikes Hodson, of Hodson's Horse, who not so long ago - September 1857 to be precise, had beheaded the sons of Bahadur Shah Zafar at Delhi, in full public view. Earlier, Hodson had started from Karnal on May 20; at dawn the next day, he galloped into Meerut, having ridden seventy six miles all night. He met General Wilson, taken a bath and breakfast, slept for two hours, and then rode back, fighting his way through some thirty odd miles of the route, lined with revolutionaries, having the unique ability to be able to sleep while riding on his horse. Hodson had died on March 11, 1858 at Begum Kothi, Lucknow in a freak incident.

Perhaps MacDonnel had been day dreaming about his role model, Hodson's exploits, when all of a sudden, in the descending darkness of the evening, there was a sudden whoosh, and a cannon ball whizzed past his head. No one really knows what followed, because in the very next moment, the air was filled with the war cries of the revolutionaries as they hacked at the British soldiers, having surrounded them from three sides, the fourth side being a deep ditch. This unforeseen assault, occurring in a typically tranquil rural area, dislodged the British forces, causing them to succumb to panic and lose their composure. As bands of Indian freedom fighters swarmed over the British troops, the dying MacDonnel had just one thought in his mind - on how to alert Outram at Lucknow about this deceptively calm area, which posed an immense threat to British soldiers, who would be marching across in this very countryside, in the coming days.

It seems that the bleeding and wounded MacDonnel somehow managed to clamber astride his limping horse at night, after the revolutionaries had retreated. The young British officer started his slow and plodding ride to Lucknow on horseback, a distance of a mere 15 miles, but unsafe and precarious - teaming with rebels and unsympathetic villagers. Just as dawn was breaking, there was consternation and panic when a wounded, limping horse entered the British lines through the Guard Post, and collapsed on reaching Outram's camp. The horse had no rider. It conveyed no message. On closer inspection of the tags, it was clear that it had belonged to an officer of the Punjab Cavalry, who had died somewhere, due to some unknown circumstances. The entire day was spent by the British in combing the country side, with some villagers even volunteering to inform that they had seen a lone British soldier on horseback at Kursi Road, moving slowly towards Lucknow at night.

When the massacre at Kursi was discovered, together with the body of the dead lieutenant, it was evident that MacDonnel had died then and there, but had somehow induced his horse to reach Lucknow to warn his compatriots about an impending tragedy. Did the spirit of MacDonnel ride the horse? No one will ever know. But the background of this incident made the British extra cautious in the neighbouring area, in Battle of Nawabganj on April 21, 1858, where about 600 revolutionaries lost their lives, but British casualties were only 67. To quote Sir Hope Grant, "A large body of fine, daring *zamindari* men brought two guns into the open and attacked us in the rear. I have seen many battles in India, and many brave fellows fighting with a determination to conquer or die; but I never witnessed anything more magnificent than the conduct of these *zamindars*."

MacDonnel's efforts, in life and death, had not gone in vain.

ЖЖЖ

The Silent Forest... Where No Bird Sang

Aghoris are devotees of Lord Shiva, represented as Kaal Bhairav, who engage in ascetic practices aimed at achieving liberation (mokṣha) from the perpetual worldly cycle of birth, death, and rebirth (saṃsāra). The Aghoris represent a significant tradition within Indian spirituality and exemplify one of the most extreme and intriguing forms of tantra. The term "Aghora" signifies light, the absence of darkness, and awareness. It also represents a lifestyle in which members of the Aghori sect maintain an indifference to the various narratives of life. It can be said that Aghora constitutes a path (sādhanā) within the framework of tantrism.

Tantra is itself associated with immorality and orgies, which reflects only its negative aspects. In contrast, the positive aspects of tantra are profoundly enlightening, offering insights and empowerment to the body, mind, and spirit.

Thakur Devendra Singh, also known as *Devender Bhaiyya* ruled over his small principality of Sairpur Khurd, between Lucknow and Sitapur, with an iron hand. He was aware of the small size of his *jagir*, but this did not deter him in any manner. The estate itself had been a gift from Nawab Ghazi-ud-Din Haider to his father Thakur Ranjeet Singh, due to the latter's loyalty and some personal obligation which had impressed the good-natured, if rather indolent ruler. The land owners of Awadh's hinterlands had traditionally maintained a love-hate relationship with the Nawabi regime at Lucknow. They preferred to stay away from the Lucknow court, being ensconced firmly inside their mud forts, deep inside jungles of thorny bushes which acted as natural barriers and moats. Paying of levies to the ruling Nawab's officials was also an exercise fraught with conflict - the visiting officials were never satisfied with the amount of taxes collected and often resorted to cruelties to intimidate the landlords. Because of this, while few paid their taxes honestly (which was never enough for the collectors), others tried their level best to avoid the exercise; some paid less than was stipulated. The more rebellious hid in the jungles and waited for the officials to return to Lucknow, the latter seething with anger and disappointment.

The same was repeated at a micro level between the landowner and landless farmers; the latter toiled all year and were forced to give up most of their harvest to the landowner, getting a mere pittance in return. Some landowners could be expansive and treated their tenant farmers fairly; others resorted to cruelties and exploitation. Thakur Devendra Singh belonged to the former category; he could not afford to antagonise the villagers of his land - any mutinous situation would have severe adverse consequences on his tiny estate as a whole. But this does not mean that the *thakur* was benevolent or sweet-natured. The landless labourers, tillers and their families were in awe and fear of their master and lord, who did not hesitate to use the whip on their backs, in case of any indiscretion. Plus, the *thakur* had a dark secret, which few were aware of. This would ultimately lead to a curse on his family and estate and eventually cause his downfall in due course of time.

Devendra Singh was a worried man. He was nearing his fifties, and yet did not have any offspring, typically a son, who would carry forth his lineage and look after the estate. His father, Ranjeet had also faced the same problem, and Devendra had been born when his father was already well past his sixties. In desperation, Ranjeet had married a young Brahmin girl of his village as his second wife, the first being barren, or so it was understood. No one ever challenged this premise and put forth the viewpoint that the *thakur* himself could be impotent. But this doubt was apparently laid to rest, when the second wife delivered a son. The furore in the *thakur's* principality subsided with time, although Ranjeet had almost kidnapped his second wife from her father's house, holding a musket aimed at the head of the unfortunate Brahmin, a *pujari* or priest in a tiny nearby temple, under a banyan tree. Few knew about the reason behind the *thakur* selecting this particular girl, and that too in this manner. Devendra's mother was not chaste and the wily old *thakur* knew of this fact. He had observed her actions for sometime, and was aware of a clandestine love affair between her and a *sepoy* or soldier of the Nawab's army, who visited the estate whenever he managed to get some sort of leave from his *paltan* or platoon.

On the day of the scandalous marriage between the old *thakur* and his nubile, if wayward second wife, the girl's paramour had been on a visit to the village. He watched in desperation and helplessness as the girl he loved was forced into this unhappy wedlock through the power of the gun. He had but one satisfaction in his mind - he was aware that the girl was already pregnant with his child. On his nuptial night, the old *thakur* was appalled when his young wife made the confession. But accepting the fact, he decided to bring up the child as his own. The child would be Devendra. It was another matter that his wife's lover was accosted by the *thakur's* men on the highway, while he was

Fig. 8: The Silent Forest of Sairpur (2021), Author.

returning to Lucknow the same night, dazed and disappointed. The unfortunate sepoy disappeared without a trace, Sairpur's dense forest of banyan trees being quite suitable for disposing off his remains.

Devendra was not aware of the circumstances of his birth - it had been a closely guarded secret. But he was familiar with a local legend about a curse in the banyan forest of his estate. It was true that not only humans, but even birds and animals shunned the area. Villagers avoided the forest even in daytime, and it was rumoured that a shimmering human figure could be seen, moving restlessly among the trees at nights. There were also reports that practitioners of the black arts had made the wooded area their haunt, knowing that they were less likely to be accosted or challenged in a place which villagers generally avoided. The huge banyan trees with their hanging roots had become immense through the centuries. They were not a source of wood, either for fuel or even for household articles or beams. As a result, the dense, ever growing forest remained dark during daytime and became quite unnerving after sunset. The setting was perfect for a new kind of horror which would soon engulf Devendra, his family and his estate.

Ram Mohan "Pyare" was the *de facto* major domo of the *thakur*. Thin as a stick, with restless, shifty eyes, a weak mouth and a crop of black hair, Pyare could go to any lengths to please his master. He had observed the *thakur's* restlessness for quite some time and was aware of his dilemma. He knew that if any tragedy were to befall Devendra, the lack of a legal heir would result in the Nawab seizing the estate, encouraged by the British authorities. An unfortunate alternative could involve the acquisition of the estate by the landlord of an adjacent estate, leading to *thakurain* Rani Sunita Devi, the spouse of Devendra, being stripped of her entitlements, while Pyare himself would be reduced to being a non-entity. Ram Mohan or "Pyare" had no moral scruples. He could go to any lengths to safeguard his interests and protect his master's estate. Being in touch with all sorts of shady, undesirable people, one day, he gathered courage to speak to his master, who was, as usual, in an inebriated state in the evening.

"*Huzoor, aapse kuch baat karni thi,*" ventured Pyare (I wish to speak something, Sir)

"*Kya baat hai? Bolo jaldi*" replied the Lord and Master impatiently (What is it? Be quick)

Pyare came closer and whispered in his master's ear about a band of *Aghoris** whom he had come across near the cremation grounds of the estate. The spiritual *Guru* of the group had assured him that a son could be born of Rani Sunita Devi, and all that was needed was a soul that would be implanted in her womb.

Pyare's cryptic talks were beyond the *thakur's* drunken comprehension. "What do you want to say? Be clear. I don't want any more nonsense from you," bellowed the old *thakur.*

Pyare realised that he was on flimsy grounds. Haltingly, he explained to his master that as per cosmic law, a soul was needed for the child to be born to the mistress. Since the master, due to his medical condition or old age was unable to impregnate his spouse; the *Aghoris* would perform the necessary rites to help get the *thakurain* pregnant. However.. here Pyare paused.

In a state of bewilderment, the inebriated *thakur* cried out, "What? What?"

"*Huzoor*, since the Master has not yet attained success regarding a male child, the *Aghoris* are prepared to offer their help in this direction. However, it requires a soul for the process of transmigration," Pyare replied with a quiver in his voice, now aware of the perilous situation he had landed himself in. Although he had been a loyal confidant to his master for many years, the terrifyingly arduous path he had chosen to make his Master happy now left him deeply uncertain about whether the *thakur* would order his execution or praise him for his efforts.

---

* Ascetics who are often found near funeral pyres, renowned for their mystical powers which are attained through their distinctive rituals, lifestyles, and beliefs. Some are believed to engage in human sacrifices, but the practice is becoming rare with time and modernisation.

On his part, Devendra was stunned into silence by Pyare's proposal. For a moment, his mind went blank, and then his intoxication slipped away like a fish slipping away from the fishmonger's slab. Regaining his logical thinking after some time, he queried, "Soul? What soul? Where will this soul come from?"

"From a human sacrifice, my Lord," whispered Pyare tremblingly, "from the sacrifice of a Brahmin or Kshatriya child, with the proper rites and incantations by the *Aghoris* would ensure that the soul, seeking another human body, would enter the mistress' womb to be her child."

"Go away! Leave me alone! Take your cursed presence away from me!" whispered Devendra, his mind and body shuddering at the dreadful implications of what Pyare had been insinuating.

Devendra entered his sleeping quarters with unsteady footsteps. His wife was already sleeping on the far side of the canopied bed. The *thakur* silently slid under the sheets; he was still trembling. He did not wish his wife to see him in this vulnerable state. But the sound of his wife's muffled weeping chilled his blood. His wife often wept by herself of late, lamenting her inability to give birth to a son and perpetuate the family legacy. Suddenly, Devendra made up his befuddled mind. He would go ahead with Pyare's suggestion, first thing in the morning, the very next day. He was now willing to take extreme measures to ensure the continuation of his legacy. Having exhausted all possibilities, he realised that there would be no further opportunities for him to preserve his estate. With his mind at peace now, he drifted into a dreamless slumber.

On hearing about his Master's decision, Pyare was overjoyed. All of a sudden, the future now seemed secure to him. Climbing on his horse carriage, he rushed off to the hide-out of Sivananda, the leader of the *Aghori* band and explained the situation to him. Nobody spared a thought that a human sacrifice of an innocent child would be involved. That those cultists would snatch away a precious life in pursuit of a horrifying ritual, the outcome of which was unpredictable. Undoubtedly, Sivananda with his matted locks and ash-smeared body presented a terrifying picture. But years of practicing gruesome rituals in cremation grounds, among smouldering funeral pyres and scorched corpses had enabled him to acquire arts, which hovered between life and death, between black and white, between good and evil. The *Aghori* leader was confident that he would achieve success with the task at hand, however ghastly it might seem to be. He assured that Pyare or the old *thakur* would have nothing to do with it; that he would obtain the child and perform the necessary rites, which nobody would observe. Only the mistress would have to come to the sacrificial site, when the rites were over, where he would bless her and ensure that his efforts had not gone awry. It would merely be a transfer of *karma.*

A week passed, and one day there was a hue and cry among the villagers of the estate. Apparently a male child, some 3 years of age - the son of a landless farmer, had gone missing while playing near the edge of the verdant forest. Search parties were organised, with Devendra himself providing his men, armed with traditional weapons to help the villagers in their search. But all was in vain. A few villagers reported that they had seen shadowy packs of wolves moving surreptitiously in the area at nights. It was supposed that the child might have been carried off by the pack to be devoured. The impoverished parents of the child were inconsolable. Getting no succour from anyone, they decided to finally leave the area and try to earn a livelihood elsewhere. Even the *thakur* did not actually associate the child's disappearance with the discussion that he had with his trusted aide, not so long ago. But he felt a chill run up his spine when a pale-faced Pyare approached shortly and requested that he should reach the hidden settlement of Sivananda, accompanied by the mistress. And that too at midnight, on an appointed day.

The meeting of the cult members with the *thakur*, accompanied by his wife, Sunita, and Pyare in tow, would be truly a night to remember - definitely not for the faint of heart. The unfortunate mistress, completely oblivious to the situation, had been merely informed by her husband that a holy man with divine powers would bestow his blessings upon her at a designated time and site, to assist her in conceiving. By the time the *thakur's* party reached the *Aghori* camp, the dreadful human sacrifice and its accompanying rituals were already over. Sivandanda appeared, his forehead, matted locks, chest and hands smeared with ash and with a red, viscous liquid. He ordered Sunita to lie on her back, near the sacrificial fire. After she had done so, the *Aghori* approached her, muttering incantations in a low, ominous voice. Dipping his hand in a small brass pot, he took a red liquid between his thumb and forefinger, smeared it on the heaving belly of the trembling lady. It goes without saying that the ashes were the burnt remains of the child's body and red liquid smeared on Sivananda and now being applied on Sunita was actually the drained blood of the killed child.

With rain clouds rumbling menacingly overhead, Sunita first seemed to go into a swoon, and then she abruptly sat up with unfocussed eyes. Uttering a loud, unearthly screech, the sound of which would echo in the accursed forest for all eternity, she thrashed her body from side to side, moaning and weeping, and starting to bleed from her private parts, obviously in the throes of an unholy abortion. As the petrified group of *Aghoris*, together with the *thakur* and Pyare watched in horror, Sunita's torment seemed to cease after some time. But with her death. Unknowingly, Sunita had been already become recently pregnant with the *thakur'*s child. As the malevolent, vengeful soul of the sacrificed child tried to enter her womb, it encountered another soul already present in a foetus, the laws of the cosmos prevented this unholy union, causing Sunita's death and liberating the trapped souls from inside her womb. The three souls, now liberated, dispassionately observed the bloody mayhem caused by unscrupulous practitioners of the black arts in the already cursed and haunted forest. The sacrificial fire went out. Sivananda staggered back, and collapsed on the ground with a thud. He seemed to be in a trance. The supernatural forces that he had called upon now turned against him, determined to make short work of this imprudent human, who had played around with cosmic forces. The *Aghori's* mind went blank and he became an automaton, neither living nor dead, all his senses blacked out one by one as a punishment for his indiscretions. His imminent death would be worse than a stray dog's and even after he died, his soul would be doomed to hover between the netherworlds forever, never attaining peace or liberation. The rest of the *Aghoris* scattered like a pack of cards, taking to their heels and deserting their camp. As if in a daze, Devendra and Pyare collected the corpse of the unfortunate Sunita and somehow staggered to their horse carriage. The events of the night would remain a secret forever and the *thakurain* would be consigned to the flames the next day, the story being that she died a normal death during the night.

But the curse that befell upon the small principality of Sairpur was just starting. It would manifest itself in many ways; Devendra would die of cardiac arrest within a year. Without a rightful heir, his estate would be forfeited by Amjad Ali Shah, then ruling from Lucknow. Pyare would be reduced to penury, dying of an unknown wasting disease, without a penny in his name. The cursed forest of the estate would remain desolate, silent, lifeless and menacing even in daytime. Wild animals of the area like wolves, foxes and jackals would howl at nights while passing by in packs but would stay away, never venturing inside. And no bird sang.

ӜӜӜ

The Haunting at Heart's Delight

In around the year 1800, after commissioning of the Farhat Baksh, Nawab Sa'adat Ali Khan, the 6th Nawab Wazir of Awadh, turned his attentions to the eastern end of the city by conceptualizing the Dilkusha (Heart's Delight) Kothi as a sort of hunting lodge, in the midst of a densely wooded area adjacent to the Gomti river. Built under the supervision of Major Gore Ouseley, the building was inspired by a country house called Seaton Delaval in Northumberland, England. Dilkusha Kothi underwent continuous modifications in the hands of its several successive, royal occupants from Nasir-ud-Din Haider to Wajid Ali Shah. Initially a hunting lodge; later it came to be utilized as a summerhouse, and occasionally as a guesthouse for visiting dignitaries. It also served as a starting point for ceremonial processions, which terminated at the Farhat Baksh palace.

The kothi was the stronghold of the Indian freedom fighters as a result of which the British relieving force, led by Colin Campbell, had to assault the building and secure it on November 14, 1857. Subsequently, the evacuees of the Residency halted here in a transit camp, on their way to Alambagh. Henry Havelock also breathed his last in this kothi (he died of dysentery), on November 24, 1857, and was later buried near Alambagh Kothi. After the British assumed control of Lucknow in 1858, a new cantonment was built on the grounds of Dilkusha, and the kothi itself was occupied by the General Commanding the Oudh Division. The building was partially demolished after 1862, although the precise date and reason for the demolition remains unknown.

With the kind of chequered history detailed above, coupled with its rather ghostly appearance even during day time, it is no surprise that Dilkusha is rife with tales of haunting. From the apparition of a British officer, accompanied by a Labrador to the tale of a murderous lady, Annabelle, who killed two British officers engaged in a duel for her affections - Dilkusha has always been less of a "heart's delight" and more about a petrifying fear of the unknown. In the following pages, we shall narrate yet another tale about this enigmatic palace complex and its grounds, leaving it to the reader to judge about its authenticity.

The story begins with Sgt. James Thomas of the erstwhile Bengal Fusiliers, who had recently arrived in India from England and was lucky enough to get accommodation in the barracks of the newly created cantonment in Lucknow after 1857. This infantry regiment had become part of the British Army in 1862 as the 104th Regiment of Foot. Prior to this, it had served for over a century with the East India Company's army. Thomas had regretfully missed out all the action during 1857-58 and was fortunate to be at Lucknow during more peaceful and propitious times. His days were spent in regimental parades, firing practice, horse riding and other mundane activities of British soldiers of those times. Being a bachelor, he would take long walks in the Dilkusha forest area, and then play a game or two of cards with fellow soldiers, before retiring to bed. Thomas was not a drinking man, but was not above taking a drink or two in the army mess, primarily for the sake of camaraderie and to ensure a restful night's sleep. But what he enjoyed most were his long evening walks in the wooded areas of the newly built cantonment. Thomas had been born in Glasgow and spent much of his youth in Manchester. He had hated the perpetual smog and intermittent rains of his home country and within a short while, grew to love Lucknow's vast open spaces and greenery. Of course, he was yet to encounter Lucknow's scorching summers, but we are digressing.

During one of his evening walks, he decided to explore the environs of the palace itself. In those days, it was occupied by the family of General McArthur, the Commanding Officer, and Thomas went up the imposing flight of steps, to the entrance of the building, which was under guard by Gregory, a fellow staff sergeant. The guard was well known to Thomas, and the two started chatting and exchanging gossip. As evening fell and night approached, the palatial building standing in all its glory presented a rather desolate look, surrounded as it was by dense forest. The army quarters we see today all around the building, some directly facing the portico of the building, did not exist in those times. Gregory, a stout Irishman with a florid complexion, then confessed to Thómas that he was not comfortable with his guard duty at the General's residence and had applied for a transfer. The Irishman did not seem to be the skittish type, hence Thomas was curious to know the reason for his discomfort.

"Níl a fhios a chara. Ní maith liom na rudaí atá ar siúl anseo tar éis luí na gréine,"* replied Gregory in rustic Irish brogue.

"Can you be more specific, Greg?" quizzed Thomas.

Gregory looked about him surreptitiously, then replied in a whisper, "I have seen things around here, which ain't normal. At about 11 pm, almost always on a Thursday, I have seen a girl in native

Fig. 9: Dilkusha Kothi shortly before demolition (1860), Unidentified Photographer.

* Don't know my friend. I don't like the things that go on here after sundown.

Fig. 10: Ruins of Dilkusha Kothi after 1862, Unidentified Photographer.

dress come from behind those trees and climb up these steps. But instead of entering, she just disappears. Her face is hidden in a veil and there is no sound of any movement when she comes."

"Now wait a minute, Greg," responded Thomas. "are you out of your mind? Don't tell me that you have been seeing ghosts here?"

"I don't care what you think, Thomas," answered Gregory haltingly, "I will go barmy if I stay around here any longer."

Thomas was perplexed. He was of sound body and mind, and his logical thinking refused to accept what Greg seemed to be suggesting.

"Look, do you want me to stay with you tonight, so we can see this apparition together? Today is Thursday." suggested the young staff sergeant.

"Sure, friend. Please stay. I shall be grateful to you forever," replied Gregory in a shaky whisper.

Thomas found a stump of a tree near the guardhouse and sat down upon it. He found Greg strangely reticent but felt it was his moral duty to support a fellow colleague and help him out in whatever seemed to be troubling him. He decided to pass the night with Greg and see for his own eyes what the latter had been telling him about.

The tropical night dragged on with the usual chirping of crickets, buzzing fireflies and the killer mosquitoes which seemed to swarm in hordes, ready to attack unsuspecting humans. Suddenly Greg grabbed Thomas' arm and whispered, "There she is! Can you see her?"

Greg's eyes were bolting from out of his head; he seemed petrified and was shaking like a leaf. Thomas looked around but could not see anything. But he thought he heard a woman's muffled scream from within the house and a hound inside starting to bark incessantly, much to the irritation of the doughty soldier.

"You really did not see anything?" asked Greg, after he had calmed down.

"Nothing at all. But what's all this disturbance from inside the house?", queried Thomas.

"It's like this every time. Once, the General even let off his gun inside the house. But I am not permitted inside, so I can't say anything for sure," replied the Irishman, now breathing normally.

Thomas scowled, clearly irritated with the ongoing unexplained phenomena in the premises. He found himself unable to unravel the mystery narrated by Greg. After bidding farewell to his friend, his thoughts in turmoil, Thomas made his way slowly along the solitary forest path leading to his barracks, uncertain of any future course of action. At that moment, his youthful zeal and logical reasoning appeared to be abandoning him.

Both the British soldiers would not know that the General and his family had been facing a terrible ordeal ever since they had occupied the official residence assigned to them. It was ironic that the Commanding Officer was expected to reside in a rather dilapidated mansion, over one hundred and fifty years old, which had witnessed numerous tragedies and political upheavals, while the rest of the army staff and soldiers had been provided with plush new housing in the recently constructed cantonment. Thomas and Greg would not know that on certain days, the General's wife would be repeatedly slapped by an unknown, invisible entity at bed time, and have her hair braids pulled viciously. Their Labrador, Caesar would let loose a volley of barks, but would not stir out of his corner to protect his mistress. In exasperation, the General had once fired his gun at the invisible assailant, but all it did was to ricochet from the wall and shatter the bedroom mirror. The "Thursday apparition" continued to appear regularly, sometimes in the children's room and sometimes in the master bedroom. With the children, it was not particularly harsh; pulling off their bed sheets or scattering their school books like a mischievous poltergeist, was the maximum chaos that it would cause. But it was particularly vindictive against the mistress of the house. The General and his family never saw anyone in these nightly attacks. They were also not aware that the guard outside their residence could perceive some ghostly figure, but was not harmed by it. McArthur was apprehensive that he might become the subject of ridicule within the cantonment; given his position, he could not afford to take the risk of confiding his problems to fellow officers.

This story of Dilkusha had its origins from the summer of 1830. The palace was a bustling place during Nawabi rule, ornate and richly furnished from inside. The entry of the ruler was not from the front but by a flight of steps from a wholly private arched entrance at the rear. The frontage, with its colonnaded portico, was used to welcome dignitaries, who would later accompany the ruler on hunts or simply attend lavish luncheon parties. The ruler, accompanied by his women folk from the harem never rode down to Dilkusha on horseback or carriage. Instead, they would sail down in luxuriously accoutred barges down the Gomti river, be received at the riverfront jetty of the royal gardens or Vilayati Bagh, and be escorted to the palace in *palkis* (palanquins). A multitude of attendants lived in another building complex adjacent to the main *kothi*. The kitchens and stables were also nearby, but at some distance away from the palace.

Although keeping British officials in good humour was the intention of every Awadh ruler, one particular unsavoury incident cast a shadow over this practice. A senior British official (name withheld) of the East India Company was once visiting Lucknow on Calcutta's orders and was provided accommodation at Dilkusha *kothi*, as per his status. The ruling king, Mohammad Ali Shah wanted to keep him away from the Residency, which was a hotbed of politics during that time. This unnamed British officer developed a fancy for a maid servant, Asma who had been assigned to take care of the personal needs of the visiting dignitary. We cannot say if Asma had similar feelings for the *gora Angrez*, but she did not refuse his overtures. The lustful officer asked her to come to the palace at night to visit him, which was an impossibility. The only day when she could be away from her household was on Thursdays, where religious festivities were held at nearby *mazar* (shrine on the grave of a holy man), and Asma would lie to her parents that she would be going to the *mazar* and listen to *qawwallis* (devotional songs) together with discourses of saints. The days become weeks and weeks became months. The British officer enjoyed the visits of Asma, who would creep inside the palace on Thursday nights and the two would enjoy the pleasures of illicit love.

This prolonged stay of the British official at Lucknow troubled the king, and the latter sent feelers to Calcutta through his prime minister, to have the officer recalled, since there was no particular reason for such an extended visit. The office of the Governor General capitulated and ordered the gentleman to return immediately. On hearing this, Asma, who by now was pregnant, raised a hue and cry. The palace, which would normally be silent at night, was filled with her sobs and lamentations. No amount of empty words could console her, and she made as if to grab the officer's gun lying on a table nearby and shoot herself. In the scuffle, the gun went off and the bullet went through her head, killing her instantly. The shocked British officer was left with Asma's dead body, which was spilling blood all over the floor.

On hearing the sound of the gunshot, echoing in the silence of the forest, the servants and attendants rushed inside the mansion and saw the bloody scene before their eyes. Stunned into silence and inaction, they went into a huddle on what should be done next.

There was no way that the news could be given to the king in the dead of night; telegraph or telephones did not exist then. The British officer cowered in the corner, as the head of the servants directed that he be tied with a rope and imprisoned. But better sense prevailed and the disposal of Asma's body in secrecy was of prime importance. The girl's body was wrapped in sheets, taken to some distance away inside the forest and buried in a hurriedly dug grave. It is another matter that the shallow grave was shortly defiled by jackals in the forest and the corpse was devoured by the scavenging animals.

When the king came to know of this scandalous story, he was horrified. Being benign and guileless, his heart wept for the fate of the innocent girl. Providing substantial compensation for her unfortunate parents, he then turned his attention to the petrified British officer and had him escorted to Calcutta, under guard. The British Resident at Lucknow did not get an inkling of this unsavoury affair and Calcutta, too was not eager that this scandal should become common public knowledge. As time passed by and Asma was forgotten, the locals would often tell the story about a wraith like figure female hovering near the Dilkusha on Thursday nights. She caused no harm to the local populace, but things changed for the worse with the British finally assuming control of Lucknow. The restless, disembodied spirit, it seemed, could not tolerate the presence of Europeans in the vicinity, and so started its vicious campaign against the General and his family, who were the first occupants of Dilkusha after 1857.

By 1860, the palace had acquired a malevolent reputation, although nobody talked openly about the actual reason for its sinister appearance and notoriety. McArthur died of a wasting disease and his family returned to England, broken in mind and spirit. Their dog, Caesar had died long ago. It was buried in a shallow grave in the compound of the building. The British army authorities thought it best to decommission the *kothi,* by demolishing it partially. A beautifully designed building, it would serve no purpose by razing it to the ground. The front of the building was cordoned off, so the building could now be approached only from its rear entrance. The spirit, if the story is to be believed used to enter the building from the front entrance, which was now off bounds. But time added a new dimension to the tragic story of Dilkusha. It was now reported that a British officer, in full army regalia, and accompanied by his Labrador, would be seen in the premises on Thursdays, obviously searching for something. And the night-long baying of an invisible hound gave sleepless nights to many living in the vicinity, which we shall discuss in another story.

ЖЖЖ

The Engine Driver

The Anglo-Indian community has long been associated with the Indian Railways. During colonial rule, the British, who had introduced the railways in India, remained more or less confined to planning and management, whereas the Eurasians or Anglo-Indians were responsible at operational levels, which included the construction, staffing, maintenance, and actual running of trains throughout the sub-continent. For more than a century, this community proudly served as the foundation of the complex network that facilitated movement across the country by railroad. Frequently, multiple generations of Anglo-Indian families were engaged in diverse positions within the railways, including roles such as guards, ticket collectors, foremen, firemen, technicians, and locomotive drivers.

Although the allure of the railway services might have diminished over time, it is well-accepted that the life of the railway worker has always been a challenging one since the very inception of the railways, and this remains true even today. From the workshop foreman to the station master, and notably the engine driver and guard, each individual confronted monotony, demanding schedules, insufficient rest and meals, neglect of family responsibilities, and occasional dangers with remarkable composure, as if they had resigned themselves to their fate. In return, the railways provided job stability, a degree of illusory prestige, status (particularly for senior officials), subsidized housing that ensured a stable life for families despite the frequent absence of the employee, as well as a measure of security through pensions and compassionate appointments in the unfortunate event of the primary wage earner's demise. These factors contributed to the phenomenon of entire families dedicating themselves to railway service across multiple generations, despite the less than ideal conditions faced by railway personnel.

During colonial rule, the first railway line constructed in Lucknow district was from Lucknow main railway station at Charbagh, close to Rae Bareilly road, passing through Bijnaur *pargana* and reaching Cawnpore (Kanpur), built by the Indian Branch Railway Company. It was opened on April 23, 1867. The Oudh and Rohilcund / Rohilkhand Railway broad gauge (BG) company was formed in 1872 with its headquarters at Lucknow, as a new *avatar* of the Indian Branch Railway Company. The Company connected Lucknow with Hardoi, Bara Banki to Chandausi and Moradabad.

Fig. 11: A Train Accident in Colonial India, Unidentified Photographer.

The Rohilkund and Kumaon Railway was a metre gauge (MG) railway company which also operated from Lucknow, providing connectivity with Kathgodam, in the sub-mountainous region of the then United Provinces. Unusual happenings occurred during the laying of BG railway tracks from Lucknow to Cawnpore (Kanpur) *via* Unnao, which we shall discuss now, gleaned more from word of mouth than from official records.

The village Mungulwar (present day Magarwara), in Unnao district, between Lucknow and Cawnpore was characterised by an undulating terrain and a significant ditch or scarp on which the tracks had to be laid. This landscape required the construction of a culvert and a minor bridge before the railway line could progress towards Cawnpore. The newly constructed bridge, despite the exceptional expertise of British civil and military engineers, experienced two collapses on the nights of the same day they were officially completed. The confounded engineers found themselves in a challenging situation, as applying the same principles to reconstruct the railway bridge appeared impractical, despite the absence of any apparent engineering flaws in the design. With the government urging for the prompt completion of the railway line and the railway company at their wits' end on how to find a viable solution, the issue was deliberated at multiple levels, yet no resolution seemed forthcoming.

In an informal discussion with local inhabitants, a British engineer, Weston was advised that the ditch or scarp in the area was "cursed", but if the angry "spirits" were propitiated by lighting a lamp and incense sticks, and a *chadar* (sheet) be spread over a mound nearby, the matter at hand could be controlled. Weston, who was Indian-born, did not scoff at this suggestion. Instead, he carried out the instructions to the letter, without divulging anything to his colleagues. The next day, he suggested to his immediate superior that one last attempt should be made to erect the bridge, and if this attempt also failed, then the tracks would have to be shifted far off, to avoid the area altogether. The work commenced, and bridge was completed. It did not come crashing down, like its predecessors. Nothing more was heard of this incident and the work of laying the tracks progressed with satisfaction. In a few months, the first train would cross over this section which was purportedly "cursed."

We now come to the travails of George Walter, the engine driver, who had been recently transferred from Jamalpur to Lucknow.

George loved Jamalpur; he had been born of a British father and Indian mother in Monghyr and had been working for the railways since youth, following the footsteps of his father, who was a foreman in the Jamalpur railway workshop. George, on his part had surpassed his father, becoming an engine driver, responsible for the movement of goods in the Allahabad - Jubbulpore (present day Jabalpur) and Calcutta to Mirzapore (present day Mirzapur) sections. He was considered to be a very efficient and able engine driver, immensely fit to drive the new rake, this time of a passenger train on a new railway line. But the man was not interested. George wanted to continue at Jamalpur, enjoying his short holidays either at Asansol and in Calcutta, or even in the cool climes of Ranchi, when it was sizzling hot everywhere. He had no desire to be stationed at Lucknow, which by then, was detested by both the British and Eurasians alike, for its role in the events of 1857. But fate had other plans. George was warned that if he did not heed to orders, his railway job could be at peril. And thus George began his lonely run from Lucknow to Cawnpore, twice a day, with short breaks in between.

George was not aware of the "cursed" culvert or its neighbouring bridge and its malevolent origins. Six months went by, with the engine driver following his dreary routine, together with the guard, Thommason. The duo shared camaraderie during their short rests between the plodding journeys. During the last return trip from Cawnpore to Lucknow, it would be late in the evening and the men would observe the lights twinkling in the homes of the villages as they chugged along, in an almost empty train. A twinkling light could also be seen on a certain mound near a certain railway bridge, which continued for many months and then, all of a sudden, was not seen anymore. One cold winter evening, as George was crossing Unnao, on his way to back to Lucknow, his empty train halted with a jerk on the Mungulwar bridge for no apparent reason. Looking down from his perch in the engine, he could see the yawning maw of the dip in the land over which the train stood stationary. Straining his eyes to look around him in the darkness, he thought he could see teeming soldiers, both in Indian and British attire. Some carried guns, some brandished swords, while few waved flags. But these were wispy wraiths, certainly not human. He thought that he could discern sword fights among the Indians and the British, but nothing was clear to his vision. Phantom cannons also fired in the air, creating havoc and bloodshed, but the scene was so illusory that George could not decide whether he was actually witnessing a phantom battle or whether he was somewhat drunk and imagining things, an ill-effect of the rum that he had been swigging from his hip flask to keep warm. While all this was going on, there was a sudden jerk and the bridge began to give way, splitting slowly from the middle. The train hung in mid-air for precious seconds and then went crashing down into the escarpment. The last conscious thought of George, before his untimely death was not about the phantom soldiers but his beloved Jamalpur, where he had spent the best years of his youth. And then his life went out like a snuffed-out flame. At the other end of the train, Thommason was luckier. Unlike George, he was not inebriated. With his wits about him, he left the guard's rear cabin and quickly jumped down, landing with a thud on the grassy land below. Other than a broken leg, he suffered no major injury as he observed with dismay and horror, how the bridge split into two and the train crashed down, its carriages disengaging and scattering in the dark countryside.

Neither George or Thommason would know that the area had seen three furious battles between the Indian revolutionaries and General Havelock's forces during July and August, 1857. There had been significant casualties on both sides, and the unfortunate men who perished in the warfare were not destined to get proper funerals. The railway men would not know that the mound over which the lamp and incense sticks had been lit was but an artificial one, containing corpses heaped on top of each other and loosely covered with soil. That the restless, vengeful spirits of the dead men would never allow a railroad, with its noisy engines and carriages, to cross over their remains and disturb their eternal sleep, but they had been temporarily pacified by the respectful act of lighting a lamp, incense sticks and laying of the customary *chadar*, a practice prevalent in the area as a mark of respect for the graves of dead saints. That after the bridge was complete and movement of trains had commenced, the locals neglected to follow their own earlier advice to Weston on how the vengeful spirits could be kept at bay. And then all hell broke loose; the tragedy had been just waiting to happen.

The railway company offered an appointment on compassionate grounds to Emma, George's young wife. But as per rule, it would not be at par with George's status, but on a much lower category - as that of an office clerk; it would prevent her from starving; but it would certainly not provide her the prestige that George had enjoyed during his service career. The reader might wonder at the injustice of it all. But then, that is life. Without logic or justification of what is right and what is wrong.

Post-script: On November 26, 2024, a British-era railway bridge near Kanpur (Shuklaganj) collapsed, due to cracks developing in piers numbered 2, 10, 17 and 22. The bridge, which extended over a length of 800 meters, had been constructed in 1874 by the Oudh & Rohilkhand Railways, under the supervision of the resident engineer, SB Newton and assistant engineer, E. Wedgard. Having functioned for approximately 150 years, the structure exemplified the durability and mechanical integrity, characteristic of colonial engineering from that period.

ЖЖЖ

The Hound

The first formal British army cantonment of Lucknow, colloquially known as Paltan Gaon came into existence during the reign of Sa'adat Ali Khan, the sixth Nawab of Awadh, in a area called Madiaon, in the outskirts of Lucknow. This was plundered and set on fire in 1857, resulting in its abandonment.

1862 saw the establishment of the new cantonment, this time in the Dilkusha wooded park of Sa'adat Ali Khan (discussed earlier), encompassing about 7000 acres. This new British cantonment comprised bungalows designated for officers, barracks for soldiers, commercial zones, places of worship, and the military area, which accounted for nearly 90% of the total site. It is extant today under the Central Command of the Indian Army.

After regaining control over Lucknow in 1858, the first priority of the colonial government was to implement a militarization strategy for the city, aimed at averting any potential insurrections in the foreseeable future. The army called the shots (pun intended) holding predominant authority in the administration and making critical decisions, while the civilian administration and bureaucracy played second fiddle, by assuming a subordinate role. Therefore, it is no surprise that the new army cantonment at Lucknow had all the accoutrements for a luxurious lifestyle for its inhabitants, whereas the civilian officials had to make do with crumbling Nawabi properties for use as their offices and residences. And yet, claimants for housing were more than the actual accommodation at hand, as more and more officials, both military and civilian landed up in this favoured area of posting, as compared to the hinterlands of Awadh. Major Everett Jameson was fortunate enough to promptly corner a prized bungalow in the new cantonment, on his arrival from Leicester (East Midlands), England; his wife and young child were to join him afterwards.

The bungalows of early British cantonments were invariably constructed from brick or stone, having a plain whitewashed exterior. Symmetrical in shape, the layout included a central hall, with rooms flanking either side, a veranda with a colonnaded portico at the front that overlooked the garden, occasionally extending along both sides as well. The roof was designed as either hipped-gabled or flat, and would be thatched, or covered with thatch. The kitchen and servant quarters would be situated at some distance away from the main building. Other additions included stables, kennels and chicken coops. The bungalows were provided with substantial lawns in the front and grounds at the rear, the latter often being used as kitchen gardens. Everett's assigned residence in Lucknow's fledgling cantonment was no different.

Fig. 12: Vintage view of a military bungalow in Lucknow, Unidentified Photographer.

As a forced bachelor, Everett did not evince much interest in his new lodgings. This was despite being provided by a retinue of native servants, including a gardener, cooks, a helper, stable boys and other menial attendants, including *punkah coolies*. He would spend much of his time in the regimental mess, when he was not on the parade grounds - his new found home being merely a place to sleep at night. The major was a tall, lanky and taciturn soldier. Back in England, he liked his evening sherry and he liked his sleep. But sleep eluded him in Lucknow. In fact, Everett had begun having sleepless nights immediately after his arrival at Lucknow. Initially, he attributed this to the drastic change of climate and lifestyle in a tropical city. He started depending on generous libations of sherry after dinner to help him fall into an alcoholic stupor. But sleep still eluded him. Eventually, the major started to attend his official day-time duties with red, swollen eyes and an unsteady walk, which did not go unnoticed by his colleagues and superiors. But nobody bothered to comment - in fact, many of them had their own problems. Everett's condition continued to deteriorate.

During one such sleepless night, his mind befuddled with liquor, the major thought that he could hear the ominous baying of a hound far away. In fact, he could not decide whether it was a hound or even a wolf. Listening carefully, Everett decided that it was likely to be the howl of a wolf, and getting up unsteadily, he first went to the gun rack, hoisted his Winchester repeater on his shoulder, and opened the front door, ready to confront whatever was creating a disturbance in the night. But he could not see anything. After straining his eyes at the darkness for some time, he walked back unsteadily to his bed. Surprisingly, he enjoyed a sound night's sleep after that night's incident.

The next night, Everett decided to take it easy with the liquor so that his senses remained alert, in case any wild animals, including wolves were prowling around his house after sundown. That night, the baying again started at around 2 am. Everett, of course, was wide awake as usual even at that unearthly hour. Springing up from the bed and grabbing his rifle, the pocket of night gown stuffed with spare shells, the major rushed to the front door and flung it open. As expected, there was nothing to see or hear. But the baying was louder and closer, *coming from the rear of the house*. Everett slammed the front door shut, and rushed to the back door, flinging it open. The baying sound was much louder here but nothing could be seen in the pitch darkness. The soldier let loose a volley of shots at the darkness, hoping to either kill or wound whatever was stalking the grounds of his house. The shooting had no effect; the baying continued for some time then faded. Alarmed by the sound of shots, Everett's servants rushed outside from their lodgings. Their hearts were chilled on seeing the major in a dishevelled state, waving his gun in the darkness and shooting at some nameless enemy. They had already observed that their master had a drinking problem but this was a bit too much. Strangely, they had not heard the baying, which had been bothering Everett of late.

On the third night, the baying was louder and closer, and on the fourth consecutive night, the baying of the nameless creature was right outside the door in the rear of the house. It was almost as if the creature had gathered the willpower and strength to come closer and closer to its victim, and was now ready to claim its prey. Until now, the proud Englishman had not disclosed this problem to either his colleagues or his servants. He was confident that he was much stronger and tougher than his unknown adversary and did not feel the justification in discussing this peculiar situation with anyone. It was another matter that none among the multitude of servants who resided on the grounds had ever heard this mysterious baying. Everett got up from his bed slowly, with confident steps, his mind completely clear and free from any intoxication. He shouldered his gun, checked the spare shells and padded soundlessly towards the rear doorway. The baying outside was tremendously loud and ominous, but Everett, confident in his own bravery and soldierly quality, gently and soundlessly opened the rear door, expecting some wild animal to pounce on him. But the dark night was peaceful outside. The major stood for a long time, his gun cocked and ready to blast the enemy, but other than the chirping of crickets and the croaking of frogs, there was not a whisper in the dark, tropical night. Shutting the door gently, the doughty soldier walked back to his bed and fell into a sound sleep almost immediately.

It was the seventh day of this mysterious phenomenon. Everett had almost started welcoming the nightly disturbance around midnight. At least he could enjoy a good night's sleep after this. He no longer felt the need to go outside or shoot at any trespasser. Instead, he continued to lie on his bed, his eyes wide open as the baying got louder and louder, reaching the back door, after which it fell silent. Everett imagined that some kind of brutish wildlife might be prowling silently outside the bungalow, unable to get inside, and would soon retreat. He did not feel the need to open the door and brandish his gun at whatever was menacing the premises for the last one week. With these placid thoughts in mind, Everett dozed off, but after some time, he awoke with a jerk. A rank, putrid smell pervaded the room and as his eyes adjusted to the darkness, he could feel his heart freeze in shock. A massive hound, its slavering jaws dripping with saliva, loomed near the bed, its eyes shining with an unearthly glow. The creature advanced toward the bed with deliberate slowness; its mouth gaping wide, before it suddenly lunged at the defenceless human sprawled on the bed. With its two front paws pinning the victim's chest, the beast's jaws clamped down on Everett's throat, ruthlessly and silently seizing the jugular, causing blood to erupt in violent spurts. The struggling Englishman, caught in the liminal space between life and death, succumbed painlessly, without even knowing the cause of his meaningless death.

Everett's corpse was found the following day by Ram Gopal, his man Friday. There were no visible injuries on his body, yet his lifeless eyes were wide open, suggesting that they had witnessed some indescribable horror sometime during the previous night. Curiously, his right hand was firmly clutching a piece of worn leather, most likely the remnant of a dog collar.

Post-script: The wooded gardens of Dilkusha, with its Kothi or Manor had been created by Sa'adat Ali Khan, the sixth Nawab of Awadh, as a sort of hunting lodge. The Nawab's favourite hound, Sheru, always accompanied his master during the hunts. However, it was killed in a freak accident with stray grapeshot during one such hunt. The ruler was inconsolable; he had Sheru buried in the Dilkusha grounds and even had prayers offered over the grave.

Dilkusha grounds underwent many changes under the successive rulers of Awadh, but was finally converted to a military cantonment by the British, post 1857. Sheru's unmarked grave came to be located in the backyard of a colonial military bungalow. It was sheer bad luck that Major Everett was allotted this very bungalow in the cantonment, soon after his arrival from England.

ЖЖЖ

A Friend Comes Calling

The owner of a car showroom in Lucknow encounters something from out of this world, in the most unusual of circumstances, proving that supernatural phenomena need not be confined to Gothic buildings, forbidding-looking ruins, cemeteries, graveyards and other ominous locations; they can make their presence felt in the most mundane of places.

Despite being the owner of a rather prestigious car showroom in Lucknow, I was never interested in attending the shindigs that the parent car company organised annually for its stakeholders. The venues would usually be starred hotels in Goa or Jaipur (occasionally Bangkok or Pattaya), the food would be sumptuous and drinks would flow like water. Souvenirs would be generous and the cultural evenings aimed to overwhelm the senses. Although there were some presentations on sales figures and future projections, coupled with rewards for best showrooms and their owners, with few Page 3 management gurus exhorting people to remain positive and be happy, the 2 - 3 day proceedings were basically jamborees with sashaying hostesses, where everyone had a good time. I could never understand what the company (or similar companies) achieved through these lavish exercises. At the ground level, sales or servicing of cars were neither based on banquets nor Power Point presentations; these were based on public perceptions, which for the Indian mindset, primarily included mileage and re-sale value. Of late, third-party influencers had entered the fray through social media, and some had regrettably succeeded in swaying public opinion, talking glibly of torque values, rpms, wheel bases, power trains and trims. Having other interests in life, I stayed away from it all, deftly passing on the responsibility of attending the annual events to the showroom manager, or even the technical manager. I accepted the fact that despite the hype, my employees were stressed out and poorly paid and that they deserved a break from time to time.

The incident which I shall relate is not a recent one. But its memory disturbs me even now. In those days, my business (and showroom) was new, and so was I. Naturally, I wanted to grasp the ropes of the trade as much as possible and had decided to personally attend one such annual meeting described above. The venue was a private yacht off the coastline of Mumbai. Although more of a cruise - the luxury yacht, *The Ayesha*, was anchored at sea - it did not sail. The crowd of attendees was impressive, and we were made to board the ship by way of small speedboats, a few at a time, the salty sea spray making us wet. But it was all good fun. Remember that I was young then and full of *joie de vivre*. Life was good, the future was bright. We were provided individual cabins, which were well equipped, having single occupancy and a view of the sea. On a rough estimate, there were about sixty attendees of my category (showroom owners / managers), coupled with company officials, many of whom had arrived from abroad. After welcome drinks, most of us preferred to retire to our cabins for a quick nap, while some preferred to lounge about on the decks, trying to socialise (which was a difficult task, seeing the heterogeneous nature of the group) in the milieu.

"Prashant?" Someone gently nudged my elbow, while I leaned near the railing, trying to enjoy the humid, rather unpleasant breeze wafting from the Arabian Sea.

I was surprised. Who could have recognised me among this sea of strangers? The person at my side was chubby, very fair, of medium built, having prominent curly almost frizzled hair. He seemed vaguely familiar, although I could not place him immediately.

"I am Kamal, from our old school days" he further hazarded, "Can't you recognise me?"

A flood of memories then swamped me. This was my old school buddy, from Class 3! Heck.. we had studied together in primary school, then moved on to another senior secondary school. Although later in different sections, we had never lost touch with each other, and would invariably exchange a few words during the class intervals. Of course, we had continued to visit each other's homes and play an occasional game of *gully* (street) cricket on Sundays. What had happened to our innocent schoolboy friendship? Why had we drifted apart, without even a word of goodbye? The sad truth was that after our board examinations, life had become hurly-burly for us kids, faced as we were with an uncertain future and very few viable career options. Some continued to study in the same senior secondary school with long-term goals but faced the loss of a year, school sessions being from January to December, while all other academic sessions in the country at university and professional level slated from mid-year. Few, like me, had left the school and opted for state-level boards, thereby saving a year, but spoiling our academic records due to sudden changes in syllabi, paucity of books in the English language, coupled with long, essay-type question-answers, which fetched relatively low marks, as compared to ICSE which had an objective, multiple-choice question-answer system. A middling number made up their minds to appear for entry in the defence services and impatiently waited for a notional class 11 to be completed so they could apply for the NDA examination.

Another motley group of students, mostly from business class backgrounds, had a lackadaisical approach, knowing that they would invariably join family businesses, where formal education with high marks did not hold much value. Kamal, from a prominent Sindhi family of Lucknow, belonged to this category. He had been destined to join his father's business of automobile spare parts and perhaps diversify it further, his fate was sealed even before he was born.

"Kamal, my dear friend!!" I exclaimed, embracing him heartily. "What a surprise to see you here!!"

To cut a long story short, we spent the afternoon and entire evening together, reminiscing over the days gone by. We discussed the past animatedly, remembering our families, common friends, and common enemies. Time flew by and soon it was time for dinner. My old friend was just as he had been as a schoolboy, being blessed with an amiable, affable temperament, although the lines of age had now appeared near his eyes and lips, which now drooped a little. Although he talked breezily, he occasionally appeared to be lost in the middle of a conversation, his gaze drifting past me as if trying to peep into the future. Of course, it could all be my imagination. Maybe he also found me forgetful and lacking in that raw energy that so characterised us in our school days. Apparently, he had found his father's business somewhat stifling and lacking in opportunity. As could be gauged from his words, he preferred to diversify in a related field, ultimately setting up a full-fledged car showroom, but in a neighbouring smaller city, to cut costs.

Time flew by in a blur of colourful events. Extravagant spreads, dance music, loud announcements, tall claims, and expensive liquors swamped the senses. Eventually, it was time to part, and as we delegates prepared to leave, there was a flurry of goodbyes and promises to keep in touch. New friendships had been sealed, old ones have been reaffirmed; since Kamal and myself shared a special bond of friendship, our parting was a bit sentimental. However, as I disembarked from the yacht, my old friend was nowhere in sight. But that was understandable. Everyone was in a hurry to leave and there were not as many speed boats for everyone to reach the shore in one go. Already the past few days seemed to be an illusion. We would be back to our humdrum lives of motor vehicles, their internal mechanicals, their features, and the perceived drawbacks of other comparable models. It was a remorseless world after all.

Time and tide wait for no man, goes the adage. I was back in Lucknow, after having a glimpse of glamour and the power of money. Strangely, it had left me rather unmoved. Deep inside me, I had accepted the fact that it had all been illusory. Hence, without wasting time in retrospection, I plunged into the world of cars, cars, and more cars. Regrettably, I could not keep in touch with Kamal, who had completely vanished after the event had concluded. I remembered him fleetingly, but those days were devoid of instant messengers and internet calls from smartphones. Talking to someone in another city meant booking a trunk call at night, which was tedious, tiresome, and expensive. No one booked trunk calls to chat - they were booked only in dire circumstances, especially to announce deaths. It was a depressing scenario, but we all survived somehow.

Time went on, and I diversified into newer business ventures. Within a decade, more and more international car brands entered India due to globalisation. Although the competition was intense, I did not let go of my showroom but preferred to employ staff with specialised qualifications, either in sales management or automobile engineering, to handle the day-to-day functioning of the business, which was slow, but not quite dead. Then came a day when the realisation hit me about my incompetence and lack of expert knowledge of my own business, due to my own complacency. It was a depressing thought, but out of sheer coincidence, on that very same day, I received an invitation for the same annual sales event from the parent car company, once again in Mumbai. This would not be on a cruise ship - this time the venue would be a starred hotel near Juhu Beach. All of a sudden, I decided to shake off my lethargy, attend the event, and instead of being just a passive owner, actually be part of the business once again. Perhaps I would catch up with others in the same rut and learn from them, or maybe I would get some fresh ideas to infuse into my own lethargic system.

Starred hotels in metro cities of India have their own USP. The ambience would be aimed to overwhelm the senses, although the food would invariably be mediocre. It would be a private world, designed to overawe, nestled within the normal world of lesser humans. As I checked in as a delegate, welcomed and escorted to my suite, I was aware that the feeling of opulent luxury was transient. A tragic real world, full of grime, heat, and dust waited outside. But my philosophical thoughts vanished in the evening when I opened the door to my suite in the evening after getting a gentle tap. And lo behold!! It was my friend Kamal standing at the threshold, looking at me with the same affectionate eyes.

"Hey dude, WTF man!!", I exclaimed loudly with delight. "How did you track me here? And where have you been all this time?"

Kamal was not as genial as me, and when I moved forward as if to embrace him, he deftly moved away and entered my room, preferring to sit in the corner on a chair. After a rather desultory, one-sided conversation, where I spoke and he listened, it was time to join the others in an "ice-breaking session" followed by cocktails and dinner. The banquet hall was crowded with the usual corporate-style seating arrangement. Kamal, who sat near me at the same table, appeared to be lost in his thoughts. The evening was colourful, the music loud, the hostesses skimpily dressed and there was this general feeling of bonhomie, when the effusive host suddenly requested the delegates to share their thoughts and expectations from the programme which would start in earnest from the next day. Two nubile hostesses moved among the tables, offering microphones to those who wished to speak. Unexpectedly, I found a microphone thrust across my face, with the hostess smiling saucily, "Sir .. would you like to say something?"

I found myself tongue-tied. I had nothing to say actually, but then, out of the blue, I started speaking:

"Ladies and gentlemen, it is indeed my pleasure and privilege to be present in this wonderful gathering, full of wonderful people. But I will not bore you with business talks - I am sure that we shall have enough of those from tomorrow. So I will share a personal moment with you all. This is the second time that I am attending such a gathering, and other than the business aspect, this platform gave me the wonderful opportunity to re-connect with a long lost friend from my school days, Mr. Kamal ...., who is the owner of the car showroom in..........., near Lucknow, and who is with me right here. We had completely lost touch after school and have managed to meet only twice in a few decades, that too because of these sales meetings. I thank you all for your patient hearing and wish the Event a grand success."

The audience did not seem to share my enthusiasm or moment of sentimentality. Few delegates surreptitiously looked at their watches, wanting this farce to end and the service of cocktails and starters to commence, followed by dinner. I failed to notice that Kamal's seat near my own was now vacant.

Dinner was an impressive affair but as expected, my jaded Lakhnavi palate found the food to be indifferent and commonplace. It was only when I was trying to go through a rather bland dessert, sitting in one corner of a table, that a rotund man with a florid complexion and an ingratiating smile approached me.

"Excuse me, sir, could you spare a few minutes of your time?" he asked politely.

"And why not? Please be seated and join me." I replied.

"Well, it is about a certain Mr. Kamal whom you mentioned in your speech," he said, hesitatingly.

"What of him? He must be around somewhere, I am sure."

"No, I mean how well do you know him?"

I bit annoyed, I replied, "I know him from childhood. We have been friends for a very long time."

The stranger pulled a chair close to where I sat and asked hesitatingly, "That means you don't know what happened to him in a similar sales meeting, some years ago?"

A bit apprehensive now, I blurted out, "Come on sir, no more quizzes now. Please tell me what is in your mind."

"My name is Rakesh Saini and I own a showroom in Kanpur," the stranger replied, making himself comfortable. "I knew Kamal for many years and I can tell you that he had taken substantial loans from private financiers to help finance his showroom and obtain the agency from the company. His family was unwilling to help in out in this business venture."

"And then?" I asked tersely.

Rakesh continued at his own pace, "About ten years ago, he was in dire financial straits, as his business was failing due to poor public response. The loan sharks backed by the mafia of the area had been hounding and threatening him for quite some time. As an escape route, he arrived at Mumbai, to attend a sales meeting, which had been organised on a cruise yacht called *The Ayesha*. When the event was over, and after all the delegates had disembarked, the yacht's housekeeping crew found his dead body in his cabin, wrists slashed. A brief suicide note stated, "They have found me here and there is no escape. Please forgive me." It appeared that the mafia had contacted their Mumbai counterparts and decided to do away with him in Mumbai itself, so as not to raise any suspicions back in his hometown."

I felt the blood draining from my face, as a shudder wracked through my body. An immense sadness came over me as I realised the plight of my childhood friend, who had been in serious financial trouble but could not gather the courage to ask me for assistance. His affection for me had drawn me to him at Mumbai once again, but by this time, he could not speak out - he had already left the physical world, but was doomed to haunt the place where he had given up his life, in the most tragic of circumstances.

Rakesh's voice jerked my back to the real world as he continued, "*The Ayesha* was also cursed from that day on, because after that horrible tragedy, no one wanted to lease it or hire it for pleasure cruises anymore. After rusting in the docks for many years, it was sent to the ship breakers in Gujarat. Good night, sir." With these parting words, oblivious to the state of my mind, Rakesh shambled away. I looked around the hall in a daze. But wait.. did I see a fleeting shadow resembling Kamal at the far end of the banquet hall? It was too hazy for me to draw any conclusion about what I had glimpsed. Perhaps it was a flight of fancy. But whatever had visited me in my hotel suite was no imagination. It had been a tortured soul, seeking succour from a long-lost friend from my school days.

ЖЖЖ

Nightmare At Firaq Manzil
- *A Novella*

(Reprinted from *Lucknow: Memories, Musings, Myths* by the Author)

I

2020

As one enters old Lucknow's Chowk area through the derelict Gol Darwaza, one's senses are assailed by a myriad of sights, smells and crowds, as people go about their daily routine in this old area of the city. The Darwaza or gateway has a chequered history, presumably built during the times Asaf-ud-Daula, the famed Nawab of Awadh. Chowk itself has undergone changes since it came into existence, more than two and half centuries ago. Many of the old *kothis* with *dyodhies* (traditional mansions with porches) have been torn down either partially or completely, to be replaced by garish shops and elevated showrooms equipped with marble-lined steps and shiny steel fittings, selling mostly items of clothing, jewellery and groceries. Here and there, one can see remnants of old buildings, shanties and narrow dingy lanes, veering off from both sides into the interiors of the area. The sight can be intimidating for the uninitiated.

One such lane, about two hundred meters from the gateway, on the right side, is expectedly narrow in the beginning, but widens somewhat, as one proceeds further down. At the entrance of the lane, an ancient old man, accompanied by a young boy, possibly his grandson, sits in a tiny wooden stall selling wilted flowers. His rheumy eyes and frail constitution can be deceptive; he possesses a powerful, stentorious voice and has a lucid knowledge of the area. He willingly and intelligibly explains the way to Firaq Manzil, which is situated further down in this side lane. However, no vehicle, not even a rickshaw, can enter into the narrow stretch. One has to leave his means of transport and walk down to his destination - there being no other alternative. The lane meanders, with derelict homes on either side, having low wooden doors, the wood having long gone to seed. Shallow pools of dirty water, on either side of the lane, small heaps of garbage, few prancing goats and an occasional public tap with urchins frolicking in the gushing water, do not inspire confidence.

For a person who is not conversant with the traditional private dwellings of the city from the Nawabi period, the area resembles a jumble of disorganised structures, more like cubby holes than mansions. But outward appearances are often delusory. For many of these low arches, with crumbling wooden doors, lead to former spacious residences inside, with open courtyards, mardana and zenana structures and quite possibly a personal Imambara. Firaq Manzil is one such rambling place, approachable by an elevated path leading to a gateway, which has all but toppled, but its pillars standing strong. On entering, one sees a moderately large open quadrangle, paved with stones, low roofed, colonnaded buildings on either side of the open space and an Imambara in front. The latter place of worship and congregation is better maintained than the wings on either side. However, there is nothing ostentatious. The buildings are crudely painted with lime wash in typical Lakhnavi style, with few steps leading to squat pillared verandas and high roofs. The doorways have typical Adam-style fanlights, equipped with collared glass. The left side building or eastern wing, seems to be neglected and decayed. Cobwebs hang around in the corners; tiny clumps of vegetation can be seen in the spaces between the paving and on the parapet. There is a general air of dissipation and lack of human activity. The servants' quarters, kitchens, water well, sheds and outhouses behind the main buildings cannot be observed from the front. In general, Firaq Manzil is just another old *kothi* with a *dyodhi*, among scores of others in the area. It is not a setting for something out of nightmares. So when a nightmarish horror came, it was unexpected and its forces were doubled.

2010

Fatima Nasreen had met Yusuf in Aligarh Muslim University when both were science major students; it was love at first sight. Fatima was a slight girl, moderately attractive, short-statured, with prominent crinkly hair, which she hated and tried to unsuccessfully straighten out with the usual electrical devices and by frequent visits to a dingy beauty parlour near the University gate. Yusuf was tall and broad-shouldered, his most prominent feature being an unruly shock of hair which fell over his left eye. Studious by nature, he avoided outdoor activities, but fate would later make him enter a profession where he would be outdoors, in dense forests, all through his lifetime. He was enamoured by Fatima's crinkly hair, and failed to understand her anathema towards something so attractive.

Their courtship had been prolonged and tedious. Prolonged, because they had accepted their situation with equanimity, knowing fully well that marriage was out of question, until Yusuf acquired a stable job. It had been tedious because Fatima's parents, both of whom were practicing doctors in old Delhi, were in no mood to let their only daughter waste her life over a student graduating in science - when there were reasonably good offers for her *nikah* (marriage), as soon as she completed her graduation. Fatima had been unable to fulfil her parent's desires and become a doctor herself. And now she had this unwanted romance at Aligarh. But she managed to get her way and join Masters in Botany, with Yusuf joining likewise. Yusuf drew his lineage from the old families of Lucknow and Rampur. But now, other than the lineage, nothing much remained, especially family wealth. But the youth, who had a serious bent of mind, was already preparing earnestly for the Indian Forest Service examination. This, he felt, would be comparatively easier to crack, than the tougher CSE, also conducted by the UPSC. The waiting was tedious for both of them; indeed at some point of time, the young couple had even thought of going their separate ways. But fate intervened and Yusuf was selected in the Indian Forest Service within two years. Things looked promising at last, but there were many unforeseen hurdles yet to appear.

2015

Yusuf's in-service training took him to Dehra Dun, and luckily or unluckily, he was allotted Uttarakhand cadre. He was lucky because at least he was nearer to his home state, as compared to his batch mates, some of whom were posted in the forests of Naxal-infested Jharkhand, or Tamil Nadu and Karnataka, the latter by now famous for their poachers and sandal-wood smugglers. Although Uttarakhand had no law and order problems, yet he was unlucky because the state's topography was unfriendly, 86% being mountainous and 65% covered by dense forests, many areas being extremely isolated, unapproachable, quite a few being above the snow line in winters. Accepting Yusuf's now elite status, Fatima's parents got her married to the young IFS officer in a low-key wedding ceremony, since Yusuf's parents were long dead and few of his surviving relatives, including a distant uncle in Rampur, were not in favour of anything extravagant or pretentious. A young entrant, Yusuf hardly had any accumulated leave in his service account, and could not afford to go for a prolonged honeymoon. After spending three days of leisure at Mussoorie, he hurriedly re-joined duty at Almora, with Fatima in tow. A beautiful colonial-era cottage, now functioning as the Forest Office rest house at Khagmara, served as their temporary abode.

"Fatima, have you thought how we shall manage, when I have to report for duty in the interiors of the state?" asked Yusuf suddenly, his eyebrows frowning. They were enjoying a simple dinner served by the guesthouse cook-cum-chowkidar, before retiring to bed.

"Why, can't I accompany you? Won't there be official quarters allotted to you?" Fatima responded innocently.

"That is OK, but some of these forests are really dense, with risk of wild animal attack. Also, the quarters are not exactly models of luxury. In fact, they are rustic and quite primitive in many places," replied Yusuf with a worried look, as the realisation suddenly hit him. "I do not want luxury, dear," replied Fatima, "I just want to be with you and take care of your needs while you are busy with your day to day routine."

But now, this nagging worry took hold of Yusuf. He had no illusions of leading a comfortable domestic life, once he had assumed his charge in some isolated outpost, surrounded by deep forests, possibly infested by wild animals. He was prepared to survive with bare minimum facilities and eat basic food prepared in a desultory manner by some staff of the camp, but what would happen to his young city bred wife? And God forbid, if there was some medical emergency? How could they raise a family in due course of time, unless he could manage a posting in some district headquarters, if not in Dehra Dun itself? Sensing that it would be futile to trouble Fatima with such troublesome thoughts, he finished his dinner quietly and prepared to retire to bed. But his young wife was no fool; neither was she unaware of the situation. She decided to avoid the topic for the moment and pursue the matter later. The day ended on a disappointing note for both.

2020

"Ammi, Ammi, look at me!" yelled Tahira, a doll-like child, barely three years of age, as she balanced herself precariously on the branch of a large tree in the forest department camp, near to the official quarters of Yusuf. Much water had flowed down the Alaknanda since the conversation of Yusuf and Fatima above. His postings had not proved to be so perilous after all, which had encouraged him to raise his family among the rustic surroundings. Other families in the camp formed a close-knit community and help was always at hand. Fatima smiled at her daughter, knowing fully well that the child faced no risk - she could clamber up trees without a second thought and engage in all sorts of tomboyish activities; after all, she was not city bred - she was a doughty child, born and brought up in natural surroundings, among tall coniferous trees in verdant valleys. The child attended a pre-nursery "school" in the camp itself, and led a carefree, happy life.

Yusuf's ramshackle jeep entered the residential area, and he hurriedly got down, reaching his living quarters with long strides.

Throwing a smile at the giggling Tahira, he entered his home and beckoned to Fatima to come inside. His wife was quick to note that her husband was tense and worried.

"What's the matter, dear?" she asked.

"The news is not good, Fatima," replied Yusuf with a frown. "Do you remember Rajive Malhotra, a young DFO, whom we had met during Diwali gathering last year?"

"Yes, somewhat," responded Fatima. "But what happened?"

"Well, he has been badly mauled by a leopard during one of his patrols, and is being rushed to Dehra. His survival is doubtful."

"Allah!! I pray that he should recover and live a long life," said Fatima.

"But the worst is yet to come, dear," exclaimed Yusuf. "I am being relieved to take over his charge immediately, as there is no officer of equivalent rank at hand."

"Is it so bad, Yusuf?" asked Fatima innocently.

"Well, good and bad, I cannot say, but the posting has a nasty reputation for sure," Yusuf replied. "The area is overrun with wild animals, and there is not much the Forest Department staff can do, equipped as they are with batons and nets. Guns, of course are not allowed, except in dire emergencies. And anyway, the guns are outdated and obsolete. Also.... and here, Yusuf stopped at mid-sentence.

"Also what?"

"The area has human habitations in three to four scattered villages, but these people do not like outsiders like us. Moreover, they are reputed to be practitioners of all sorts of black arts, including magic, sacrifice and worship of earth spirits for casting spells. We do not disturb them and they do not disturb us, although we are aware that they surreptitiously trap protected animals, nor for eating but for practicing magic. The community is known as *Kallu Pahari* and is shunned by other communities living in nearby villages."

"I really don't know how to respond to this, Yusuf," frowned Fatima. "In fact, I am a bit surprised that you can believe this mumbo-jumbo in this day and age."

"You belong to Delhi, Fatima," replied Yusuf gently. "You are a city-bred girl who does not understand these things. I lost my parents at a young age and grew up in a village in Rampur district, being looked after by my uncle's family. They preferred to lead a simple village life, although we had substantial ancestral property in old Lucknow. The property was reported to be cursed by an evil entity, or entities, I do not know. But I do know that the curse did not let my uncle live in peace even in his village. Misfortune and unexplainable tragic events followed him and his family throughout his life, and continues to do so even now."

"You mean that this entity or spirit or whatever, was determined to make your uncle's life a misery, wherever he went? But why?" Fatima eyes grew round at this revelation.

"I have no idea, dear," replied Yusuf tersely. "But I had thought I would be free of these things as I grew up and settled far away from family ties. But it seems, I shall face a similar problem in Rikiyasain, the land of the *Kallu Paharis*".

"Why so?"

"Because apparently Rajive had caught the villagers trying to sacrifice a sloth bear, under a tree, having a makeshift image, after beating the poor creature half dead with sticks. Rajive had confiscated the "sacrifice" and warned the wrong-doers using strong language. In response, the headman, a ruffian called Chander Rawat, had warned Rajive that he would be dead within 24 hours due to his blasphemy. And now this poor officer is fighting for his life!!"

Both Yusuf and Fatima fell silent after this discussion, each lost in his / her thoughts. Fatima did not entirely disbelieve Yusuf's story of the supernatural although she felt that the leopard attack could be a mere coincidence. Fatima was a rational woman with an open mind. She was aware that science could not explain many phenomena, and ghostly activity was one such area where science had not been able to make much headway. This did not mean that the supernatural did not exist. Most probably it did. It was alright.. as long as it did not turn malevolent and harmful, so she felt.

"Fatima, although you can stay in these quarters for some time, we would have to vacate it in due course, and you will have to join me in my place of posting," muttered Yusuf. "We have a young child and her education is just starting. We cannot keep her in such an isolated place at this stage."

"So what do you suggest?"

"I have been wracking my brains on the problem, ever since I came to know about the situation," Yusuf responded. "an option would be to send you to Lucknow, with Tahira. My ancestral property is lying vacant there. You can live there comfortably, as the opposite wing is occupied by my cousin brothers and their families. They would help you set up an establishment. Also Tahira would get far better education in Lucknow, than she would have in this remote area."

Fatima's heart fluttered with anxiety as the realisation hit her. Her life and her daughter's future were suddenly on the cross-roads. Harsh decisions had to be taken; her life was about to change and she would have to live without her husband.

"And what about you, Yusuf?" she enquired.

"I will join of course. No option there. But I will get a joining period leave, which I will use to drop you at Lucknow and help you settle there. Then I will return here," Yusuf replied.

Fatima had never been to Lucknow, although she had heard a lot about this famed Nawabi city and its unique laid-back culture. She was excited to be able to live in this city, but alone? What would her life be like? And she had a young daughter to take care of. But she possessed grit and determination, and would not let her emotions and insecurities come in the way of her domestic life. Her husband needed her support; after all they had married, fully knowing about the uncertainties that his job entailed. What would be the point of creating issues now? She therefore agreed to Yusuf's proposal, her mind already busy, planning about her impending journey and a new life-style that was fast approaching her.

II

The British-era Doon Express chugged into Lucknow's colonial Charbagh railway station sharply at 8.30 am. It was a crisp March morning. Yusuf and his family got down hurriedly from the train; their journey had been comfortable and they were raring to start a new life, far removed from forests, animals and practitioners of the black art.

"Yusuf, is it true that this train has been running on this route for more than a century now?" Fatima asked innocently.

"Since 1903 or 04, but I can't be sure, Fatima," smiled Yusuf, his mind already busy with future plans and a hundred other details one is usually confronted with, in a transfer and posting.

Their cab plunged into the crowded roads of Lucknow, heading swiftly towards the old quarter of the city. The milling crowds and traffic did not intimidate Fatima - after all, she herself was a product of old Delhi. But their young daughter seemed speechless on seeing throngs of people for the first time in her young life. Her carefree existence among tall trees, vast open spaces and fresh air suddenly seemed far away. The crowds, bright shops and tall buildings seemed exciting, but the air was stale and smog was everywhere, which made the child cough. Things would never be the same again for her.

Their approach to Firaq Manzil was intimidating, as they had to half carry and half drag their luggage, while walking up the winding lane. Once inside, they were greeted by Shoeb and Akhtar, cousins of Yusuf, who now lived with their families, in the right wing of the rambling house. Shoeb's wife, Faiza, and Kausar who was Akhtar's better half, embraced Fatima and led her inside their dwelling. Their two children, Salima and Adil, almost the same age as that of Tahira, danced around their cousin. The children were elated that they had got a new playmate. Tahira stood silently, her innocent mind absorbing the new atmosphere of this huge house with its high ceiling, arched walls and a somewhat gloomy atmosphere. The extended family gathered around a substantial breakfast, after which the nitty-gritty of Fatima occupying the left wing with her daughter was discussed.

"Yusuf, your portion of the house is vacant and it has four large rooms, including the original *dewan khana* (sitting room), as well as a huge *bawarchi khana* (kitchen) and two *ghusal khane* (washrooms). At best you can use two rooms as living and bedrooms. The other rooms can remain locked as they are. After all, it is very difficult to clean and maintain such a huge premises, when you are alone with your young child," suggested Shoeb. Yusuf nodded in agreement, but Fatima wanted to see the entire wing, before taking any decision. The cousins had managed to clean the rooms and washrooms, on their own, but the huge veranda was still dusty, with vegetation growing between the stone paving. It would take a lot of effort to make the wing spick and span, and even more effort and money to keep it that way. The kitchen was huge and dark, but with renovation and proper fittings, it would not be so intimidating. Yusuf would spend a week putting things ship-shape, aided by his cousins. An old lady from the neighbourhood had been roped in to act as a maid. An aged and decrepit gardener, who occasionally made an appearance in the property, would clean the paving, and install some potted plants in the premises.

Fatima decided to use three of the rooms - one of the rooms, the original dewan khana would be a nursery and playroom for Tahira. Her daughter was not used to enclosed spaces, and would be happier to have her own large den, in her own private world of dolls, story books and toys. The remaining last room would remain locked. On hearing Fatima's decision, Yusuf's cousins exchanged glances, but remained silent. For the next six days, carpenters, plumbers, electricians and workmen worked busily, giving the neglected wing a bright, cheerful and contemporary appearance. Yusuf had all but emptied his meagre savings bank account to pay for the work being done, as he wanted his wife and child to be comfortable and not feel deprived in any manner. After the renovation work was over, it was obvious that maximum effort and expense had been showered on

Tahira's playroom. Originally this room had been the living room or dewan khana of Firaq Manzil, appropriately equipped with heavy furniture and furnishings to accommodate visitors and guests. Now the entire room was done up with pink shaded wood-work, matching contemporary fittings, including the storage spaces, with even the ceiling fan having Disney characters painted on it's wings. It had been transformed into a little girl's room - Yusuf made sure that Tahira would not feel any pangs of depression or deprivation, on being suddenly transposed from a happy-go-lucky life to a cloistered one in a rambling old house with unpleasant memories and associations. But even Yusuf was not very well conversant with whatever ill-association the house retained within itself. He had never lived here; he was only aware of he had been told by his uncle, and his memory was hazy. Maybe it was all superstition; perhaps it was all imagination, so he reasoned with himself, as he left for the railway station to board the Doon Express once again at night. But this time he was alone. His family was safely in Lucknow, in a house done up as best as possible, under the protection of his cousins, who were staying barely an arm's length away. All was well and under control.

Yusuf had not been informed that his colleague, Rajive had breathed his last in a government hospital in Dehra, due to blood toxaemia and septicaemia, caused by his fatal injuries. He had died within twenty fours after his confrontation with the village headman, Chander Rawat, as predicted by the latter.

It did not take long for Tahira to adjust to her new surroundings. She had not yet been admitted in a formal nursery school, and her time was spent in playing with her cousins. She especially loved to play hide-and-seek in the sprawling premises, with plenty of shadowy nooks and crannies. The huge well at the back of the house fascinated her, but unfortunately, it was boarded up and she could not peep inside. However, Tahira's favourite place soon became her own den, where she would spend hours, playing with her dolls, crooning to them as if they were alive. Within a few weeks, she withdrew from her boisterous games with her cousins and seemed to be content in her own company. This development disturbed Fatima slightly, but she kept quiet. Anyhow, busy as she was in setting up her new establishment in a completely unknown city, which included Tahira's admission in a reputed school, she could hardly spend time worrying about her child's fascination for her den. After all, that had been the very purpose of providing the den to Tahira, was it not? In whatever spare time she had, Fatima, accompanied by one sister-in-law or the other, delightedly explored the famed markets of Lucknow and visited few of the better known monuments of the city, including the Residency and the Bada Imambara.

Tahira had always been a precocious child. Now, she seemed to derive a particular satisfaction of being alone in her den, even when her mother or her aunts were nearby. Tahira never felt lonely or scared. In fact, she felt secure, under the watchful protection of loving eyes, something which she did not feel even in her mother's presence. While sitting cross-legged on the floor, occupied with her toys, the child could occasionally sense a strange fragrance wafting near her; sometimes she felt that she had a playmate; however, this playmate was not another child, but someone older, a grown-up, like her mother. In her child-like innocence, once she even offered her toys to this "friend" whom she could not see, but of course, there had been no response. As the days passed, Tahira became more and more aware of the presence near her. She felt loved and protected, but she could never see anything, although she could recognise when the presence was nearby and when it was not. Her child-like logic told her that it was useless to tell her mother about these feelings. In any case, adults just could not understand the problems and feelings of little children, so she reasoned. Had her father been present, perhaps she would have ventured to discuss her experiences with him, but her mother was always busy, either with household work, gossiping with her sisters-in law, or exploring the city. Fatima had started to happily imbibe the Lucknow "feel" and was convinced that her daughter had adjusted marvellously well in her new, if somewhat cloistered surroundings. Of course, all these were only superficial, and there was much more to come.

Back in Rikiyasain, Yusuf was struggling to adjust himself to his new place of posting. This was the first time that he was separated from his family. This was also the first time that he was in a remote location, with hardly any outside contact. His living quarters were pitiable, and the enormity of his decision to join the Forest Services dawned upon him. Earlier, the news of his colleague's tragic death had stunned him. Yusuf's days were dreary and his nights lonely. Suddenly, life seemed to be a burden. Fortunately, he had not come across any member from the dreaded community that the area was infamous for. In any case, it was not their wherewithal to interact with outsiders or disturb them in any manner. They only seemed to react when thwarted or prevented from carrying out their day-to-day activities.

It was a warm sultry April afternoon, when Yusuf had a strange experience during his routine movement in the deep jungles of Rikiyasain. Earlier, he had received reports that a Himalayan black bear had been marauding the area, carrying off livestock but avoiding humans. As his jeep moved through the broken jungle path, shaking and careening, he spotted five or six locals running hither and thither, shouting hoarsely and waving sticks in the air. Obviously, the rampaging bear was nearby. Within few moments, the entire group disappeared among the trees, the forest being so dense in parts that it appeared to be quite dark, almost twilight. In his bid to prevent the jeep from running over the villagers, Yusuf's driver slammed on his brakes; the overheated engine sputtered and died. Yusuf and his team were suddenly stranded in the deep forest with a breakdown. His staffs were unperturbed and one opened the bonnet to see the cause of overheating, while others examined the tyres and brakes to see if any serious damage had occurred. For them, it was part of a regular routine. In the meantime, Yusuf's eyes had adjusted to the dim light, and he fancied that he could see a human figure among the trees. He decided to approach the person and ask for directions, as it appeared that the person actually wanted to talk to him, but away from the others.

Coming nearer, he could see a middle-aged man, in typical Garwali clothes, standing quietly among the shadows, waiting for Yusuf to be at arm's length. Despite his shabby attire and unkept appearance, he had piercing eyes and a commanding personality.

Speaking in chaste Hindi, he asked Yusuf, "So you have come to replace Rajive saheb, who insulted us and our Gods?" Yusuf was flabbergasted. In a remote place like this, where everyone either spoke Garhwali or Hindi with a heavy accent, who could be this man, speak in chaste Hindi of the plains? And how did he know about his deceased colleague, Rajive?

The stranger continued, "Saheb, you are a long way off from the plains and your own home. Your wife and child are in danger. Try to save them before it's too late."

"Whhat.. what.. who are you? How do you know all this?" stammered Yusuf.

"That is not important, Saheb. I have no quarrel with you. Our people just want to live peacefully, continuing our old traditions and customs. Our Gods do not forgive anybody who blasphemes against them, or tries to disturb us in any way," replied the man, speaking softly, yet menacingly.

"But how do you know about my personal life?" persisted Yusuf.

"These eyes see all; these ears hear all, Saheb," the stranger answered. "I did not curse your friend. I did not cause him to die. He insulted our Gods and brought the curse upon himself. I merely predicted what would happen to him due to the curse."

Yusuf remained tongue-tied before the forceful personality of this man from the deep jungles. He had this mental picture of a rustic brute, who had in some mysterious way caused the death of his colleague. But this man in front of him was no ruffian or trouble-maker. He looked sane, sober and his personality was indeed remarkable.

"I take your leave now, Saheb," continued the mysterious stranger, whom Yusuf could now identify as Chander Rawat. "But wait," the stranger paused, "as a measure of my goodwill, I give you this holy ash. Scatter it in four directions in your home. You might be protected from the evil that stalks you by day and watches you by night. I can say no more."

With these words, the Rawat retraced his steps and soon vanished into the gloom of the forest. Yusuf was left standing flabbergasted, holding a small bag tied with string, which Rawat had given him before leaving.

That night, Yusuf could not sleep. He tossed and turned - his mind in a whirl, as he tried to weigh the options before him. There was no way that he could abandon his posting and rush off to Lucknow, on an imaginary or perceived threat - that too supernatural in nature. But the welfare of his young wife and child was foremost in his thoughts. How could he solve this problem, if at all there was a problem? Suddenly he remembered the charm that Chander had presented him. Could the bag be sent to his family if he could not go himself? But how? There were no courier services in the vicinity. He would have to approach his colleagues, identify someone who was proceeding to any town nearby and hand over the bag to him, requesting him to courier it to Lucknow. The bag itself was small, possibly made of animal skin. It would have to be packed securely before being handed over. He would then phone Fatima, and ask her to scatter the contents near their living quarters. With these troubled thoughts, Yusuf fell into a restless sleep, dreaming of sacrifices, pale-faced menacing figures who were half human and half animal, and for the first time, he imagined that even in his sleep, there was a presence standing beside his bed, observing him closely, if not menacingly.

The next day, Yusuf using all his resources, could finally succeed in identifying someone who would be visiting Almora town for petty local purchases for the office. He asked his driver to proceed to the outpost, and hand over the now securely packed package to the office staff member, who had assured him that he would do the necessary job - it was a very minor one anyhow. The latter would also approach the most efficient and networked courier agency, if the courier charges were not the problem. Yusuf agreed that money was not the issue at all. In any case, the package was promptly delivered to Fatima, within four days; Yusuf had already instructed her telephonically on how to go about using it. His directions had left Fatima astonished. But she could sense the urgency in his voice and agreed to follow his instructions. Instead of scattering it in the wind (she could not understand the four directions aspect), she decided to scatter a tiny bit in each of the rooms which they had occupied, ignoring the one kept locked up. The kitchen and veranda would also get a tiny bit and be blessed, so Fatima reasoned. After cleaning her limbs, and donning fresh clothes, she did as directed, with Tahira looking on with innocent eyes. Fatima did not feel like sharing this action or discussing it with her in-laws next door. Somehow, she felt that they would regard her as an eccentric.

That night, Tahira sleeping next to Fatima on the bed, woke up with a scream. She clutched at her mother and sobbed loudly, "Ammi Ammi.. bachao.. please save me. They are taking me away.. Ammi Ammi, please.. !" Tahira's eyes were tightly closed and tears rolled down her cheeks, as she struggled with an unseen power which seemed to send her body into convulsions. The terrified Fatima held her child tightly to her bosom, trying to sooth her and console her, while Tahira continued to struggle and jerk. After a long time, she calmed down and fell into a deep slumber. Fatima could not sleep anymore that night. She kept vigil over her sleeping daughter, who twitched and murmured in her sleep, but did not once open her eyes. The rest of the night passed in this manner, and Fatima could finally snatch few winks as dawn was breaking. It was the first night of horror for them; more were yet to come.

During the day, Tahira was her usual cheerful self. She did not seem to remember anything from the previous night, and Fatima did not think it would be prudent to probe in this direction. Maybe it was just a bad dream. But in the back of her mind, her action of scattering some ashes, possibly having some magical powers could have been a reason. Maybe her attempt to "purify" the place had actually aggravated and annoyed the entities lying in slumber. It was all very mysterious, but people, including children did have nightmares, did they not? Fatima was soon busy with her household chores. She also reasoned that it was high time that Tahira ought to be in school, so she could give vent to her excessive energies, instead of being cooped up in her playroom day and night. On her part, soon after breakfast, Tahira rushed off to her den. She hardly interacted with her cousins anymore, who now regarded her as a bit of a crank.

As Tahira assembled her toy train on its tracks, checking the tracks and other fittings, before starting its run, the child was suddenly aware of her unseen "friend" who was watching her keenly. Tahira glanced behind her shoulder, then seeing nothing, turned her attention once more to the elaborate toy train set, which was equipped with a rather long and winding track, working signals, tiny stations, bridges, figures of people, grazing animals and a tunnel. The train started its run, chugging slowly at first and then gathering speed. The console was in Tahira's hands, but as the train engine and its bogies, six in number, sped along, somehow the child lost control of the engine's movement. The train ran fast, then faster, not stopping at any of the stations and started to rush forward with terrifying speed, threatening to topple over at any second. The console was non-functional and in addition to the train's scary movement, the child could now feel that the presence in her room, her mysterious "friend" was no longer friendly. It was watching the goings-on with a malice which terrified the innocent child.

The toy train, in its mad rush, did not topple, but continued its uncontrolled journey, although sparks now flew from its electric components. Tahira continued to watch all this with horrified eyes, the console held uselessly in her hands; for the first time, she could sense not one but two invisible presences observing her malevolently, their gaze drilling into her back. Somehow, they wanted this charade of the toy train to end and the child to leave the room. The child was now an interloper, a nuisance, because the room belonged to them and they wanted privacy. And they would punish anyone who went against their wishes. All these negative feelings swamped the sensitive child's psyche and unable to bear the mental strain any longer, Tahira yelled loudly and rushed out her room. She continued to scream as her mother and aunts ran to embrace her and console her in whatever way possible. "*Ammi!! Khala!!* Save me. *Mujhe bachao.* They will kill me!!" screamed Tahira and collapsed in a faint.

After Tahira had been revived, and lay weeping on the bed, Fatima ventured to the playroom to try and understand what had actually happened. Were there intruders in the room, who had frightened her child? But how was that possible? Inside the room, Fatima saw that the toy train had toppled over; in places it had caught fire. The tracks and other fittings had become disjointed and lay strewn across the floor. Other than that, there was no sign of any intruder, human or otherwise. As an adult, Fatima did not possess that ESP which could have warned her that two malevolent beings, which did not belong to this material world, were still very much present in the room, observing her balefully. She hurriedly gathered the scattered parts of the toy, stuffing them in the box, and left the room, oblivious that she too had a close shave with something that she had inadvertently aroused, through her action of scattering ashes in the premises. Ashes over which certain incantations had been read, ashes which had the power to energise and provoke beings from the netherworld, which would then act as per their nature. A gentle personality would be helpful and benign; a spiteful being would be hostile and destructive.

Yusuf was unable to clearly understand Fatima's babble, as she tried to express herself incoherently over the phone, that too over a disturbed line. However, he immediately understood that something was seriously wrong and that he would have to reach Lucknow without further ado. But considering the route and official formalities, reaching home would take at least 24 hours if not less, including an overnight journey by train. While he made preparations to leave immediately, he also sounded his cousins staying in the premises; the latter promised all help and support. In fact, after that incident, they had not left Tahira's side for a moment. A doctor had been summoned, who pronounced that the child had experienced some sort of mental trauma, but it was not usual for precocious children, who invariably had a lot of imagination and lived in a world of fantasy. He prescribed a mild sedative and Tahira was soon fast asleep, tucked up in her mother's bed.

For the rest of the extended family, excepting Fatima, the developments were not very surprising. They were vaguely aware of the history of the premises and the evil influence it harboured, especially the east wing. In fact, it was just a matter of time before something very unpleasant occurred. And it now seemed that Fatima had inadvertently precipitated the crisis through her actions. Whatever had started was expected. The house had been disturbed for over a century now, with no respite. Ill-luck seemed to follow its occupants, even after they had vacated it, and moved out of the city. Shoeb and Akhtar had continued to live in the west wing, simply because there was no other option; their combined incomes were too meagre and living in separate establishments, away from Firaq Manzil, was an impossibility. Also, the west wing appeared to be less accursed; disturbances were rare. In contrast, the east wing, where Yusuf had now settled his family, was prone to psychic disturbances, some frightening, and others subtle. But a constant undercurrent of tension always seemed to be lurking there. The presence of the personal Imambara in the premises, the obsequies observed during Muharram and the occasional visits by maulanas or holy men did not appear to deter the supernatural activity present in the east wing. Shoeb remembered what his father (Yusuf's paternal uncle) had told him about the horrifying occurrences which he had faced several decades ago, forcing him to abandon his inheritance and migrate to Rampur. Apparently Yusuf's father had also died in a freak accident, his clothes catching fire without any reason, in the very room that was now the playroom of Tahira.

The next morning saw Yusuf hurriedly arriving at Firaq Manzil, much to the relief of his family. Tahira was delighted, hugging her father tightly, her frightening experience all but forgotten. Fatima was pale-faced as she greeted her husband, and the two sat down for breakfast. Somehow, the previous day's incident seemed trivial, when narrated in broad daylight, with a warm breeze blowing in the courtyard, and birds chirping, indicating an early summer. Tahira, fully recovered and overjoyed at seeing her father, skipped to her playroom and looked around. Her toy train set was in pieces - it seemed beyond repair. Undeterred, she settled down on the carpet, bringing out her impressive collection of Barbie dolls and their elaborate sets. Time flew by, with Tahira happily cooing, completely immersed in her make-believe world of dolls. She arranged and re-arranged their clothes, kitchen accessories and sports kits. Life was fun once again.

In the veranda outside, Yusuf and Fatima continued to be deep in conversation, discussing the present situation and future course of action. Chander's ominous warning continued to haunt Yusuf - he was unable to accept Tahira's scare of the previous day as something routine. Something ominous was active in the premises - that he was sure of, but he could not pinpoint what it was. He had heard tales of this house from his father and uncle; he was also convinced that something malefic, something sinister, had been stalking his family for almost a century now. But he was unable to make up his mind, make a decision and move. He had invested his meagre savings in refurbishing the dilapidated east wing; he could not take his wife and child back to the wilderness, where he was currently posted. So what was to be done? Fatima's wan face dampened his spirits and depressed him. Unable to come to any conclusion, he looked around but could not see Tahira around. The child had now been on her own for over two hours in her den. Yusuf decided to shake himself clear of morbid thoughts and join his daughter in a playful mood. He arose, and walked to the playroom, intending to greet his daughter with a hug and a kiss. But what he saw inside the room stunned him and set his heart pounding. Tahira lay on the floor, seemingly unconscious. Her clothes were half burnt, and so were her dolls, which were scattered across the floor in different directions. However, there was no smell of burning anywhere. What petrified Yusuf and brought him in cold sweat was the expression on the face of the comatose child. It was obvious that she had encountered something so hideous, seen something so dreadful, that losing consciousness had been her body's defence mechanism, rather than losing sanity.

III

1920

The Lucknow Pact of 1916 had re-united the Hindu and Muslim communities, paving the way for Gandhiji's Non-Cooperation Movement of 1920. The freedom movement gained momentum, although Sir Harcourt Butler, then Governor of the United Provinces, known for his inclusive approach, did his best to keep a watchful eye on the various communities then living in Lucknow, including his own countrymen. The Indians were full of resentment against their white "masters", with the latter doing nothing to assuage the feelings of the native population; in fact, their attitude towards the local populace was full of contempt and condescension. A time bomb was slowly ticking away, similar to the one which had exploded nearly sixty years ago, as India's First War of Independence. The Europeans or *firangis* generally avoided the old city, confining themselves to the Civil Lines or Hazratganj and of course, inside the new Cantonment at Dilkusha. But maverick British military officers and civilians did move around clandestinely in the lanes and by-lanes of old Lucknow, for a variety of reasons, none of them good. One such officer was Captain Reginald Archer, popularly known as "Reggie" among his friends, not that he had many friends. Reggie was tall, stoutly built, with moderately good looks, a pug nose and shifty, restless eyes, greyish-green in colour. His undesirable habits and sexual predilections annoyed even his fellow officers. This army officer had got into the habit of donning civilian clothes, and moving around among the native populace, which generally avoided or ignored him. During one of his wanderings, this time in a crowded lane, known for serving spicy, barbecued food, in the Chowk area, he came across a girl, whose beauty and sensual figure were obvious, even though she wore a hijab. Although Lucknow had no dearth of female beauties, something stirred inside Reggie, which was not pure lust. He observed the girl from a distance, which he shortened by taking long strides towards her. The girl, whose name was Aatifa observed this saheb approaching and shyly lowered her eyes, preferring to clutch her package of kebabs and hurry back to her home, which was Firaq Manzil.

Reggie watched her disappear inside a doorway; little did he know that the modest entrance led to rather spacious premises inside-the house owner being Ashar Ahmed, a local, wealthy landlord and a staunch supporter of the Khilafat Movement. Aware of the atrocities that his ancestors had faced during and after the events of 1857, Ahmed hated the colonial rulers with a vengeance. His only daughter, Aatifa, nubile, yet innocent, was not aware of her family's history. She was only mindful that a gora Saheb had made eye contact with her and his pointed stare had made her heart flutter. On his part,

Reggie retreated, discretion being the better part of valour. But he had become restless now. His encounters with shady locals, including women of loose virtue had left him jaded. He suddenly had this desire of knowing this unknown girl better, on an intimate, personal level-knowing fully well that it would be an uphill task, that too fraught with danger.

Reggie returned to the cantonment, his mind in a whirl. He made a mental note of approaching his local contacts the very next day, after his regimental parade and other routine duties were over. He was aware of some Indian sepoys in his own regiment, who could be enticed into becoming informants. One such sepoy, Rafiq, already in trouble with his superiors, due to his outspoken political views, would be the best bet. This maverick sepoy could perhaps be assured of immunity against any official action against him, on the condition that he would delve into the antecedents of this nameless girl, who lived behind a modest gate, in the old city.

A month passed, with Rafiq agreeing to his Saheb's wishes and spreading his network far and wide, ultimately striking gold. One evening, greeting Reggie with a sloppy salute, which was more of a salaam, he spoke gleefully, "Saheb, I have done your work. You must give me big reward."

Reggie, who was lounging in the veranda of his official army bungalow, a glass of whiskey in his hand, stared at Rafiq with unfocussed eyes.

"*Chup karo, bakwas band karo*!!" he snapped, "*Kaam ki baat bolo*!!"

Undeterred, Rafiq went on to relate how Ashar Ahmed was in trouble as he did not have the necessary papers to prove his ownership and inheritance of the sprawling ancestral property where he resided. If Reggie could put in a good word with the local British magistrate, who would then allow Ashar to prepare and submit papers afresh as proof of his inheritance, Ashar's problems would be solved to a great extent. In due course of time, things did materialise as Rafiq had predicted. Although the sepoy did not get any benefit out of his cloak-

and-dagger operations (in fact, he was marched out of Lucknow to Agra cantonment, at the instance of Reggie's superior, a red faced Irishman named Col. MacClery), Reggie and Ashar Ahmed quickly became close friends. And this paved the way for Reggie's visits to Firaq Manzil, which sent Aatifa's heart fluttering, as she observed this dashing British officer in full army regalia, relaxing in the dewan khana of Firaq Manzil. Admiration soon changed to mutual infatuation, and both searched for a way to meet alone, far from the prying eyes of the family and community.

Reggie and Aatifa did not have to wait long. During one of his sudden visits to Firaq Manzil, that too in the daytime on an off-day, Ashar invited him to stay back for lunch. Excusing himself for a moment, Ashar hurried out to the nearby market for buying provisions, instructing his daughter to serve drinking water to their honoured guest. As Reggie lounged on an easy chair in the dewan khana, Aatifa entered the room, the anklets on her feet tinkling sweetly. Her heart fluttered wildly in her breast and her hands trembled, as she held out a tray containing sherbet and sweetmeats. Reggie gently took the tray from her and kept it on the table. While Aatifa stood before him with downcast eyes, he took both her warm, delicate hands in his own, and drew her close. Passion welled up in their young hearts, as Reggie pulled her closer, making her sit on his lap. She threw her arms around his neck, holding him tightly, while he smothered her beautiful face with passionate kisses. Their lips met, as Reggie groped her and fondled her supple breasts under her dress. Time stood still for both, as they explored each other frantically, oblivious of the dangers they faced. That moment was pure magic, but it would be torn asunder in a matter of minutes.

His purchases over, Ashar entered the dewan khana jauntily, and was momentarily stunned at what he saw. He seemed to freeze with shock, his blood congealing, then his anger and old resentment for the gora log, the firangis swamped his senses. The thought that his own daughter could be equally guilty for this indiscretion did not cross his mind, which had seemingly blanked out.

"*Lā ḫawla walā quwwat*," growled Ashar in a choked voice, and snatching a decorative sword adorning the wall, he rushed at the couple, intending to make short work of this infidel. On hearing her father's angry mutter, Aatifa's eyes jerked open and in a split second, as a reflexive action, she pushed Reggie sideways, away from her. The sword swerved, and missing Reggie's unprotected back, it entered her throat. The rush of the weapon was so forceful, and its blade so keen, that it all but sliced her head off. As she fell on the floor, blood spouting from her severed throat in great spurts, Reggie looked at his dying lover with horrified eyes, oblivious of the fact that the next swing of the sword would take his life, as it plunged into his back, severing his heart into two.

Maddened by grief, anger and self-mortification, Ashar continued to hack at the dying British officer with the sword, severing his limbs and gouging out the eyes, which had cast their sinful look on Aatifa. As the dying lovers lay on the floor, life slowly ebbing out, their blood intermixing in death, their spirits, now released from their bodies, observed their own mutilated mortal remains on the blood-spattered floor. The anguish of their unrequited love, the uncontrolled momentary passion both had experienced, and the terrible rage at being deprived of the pleasures of flesh, unleashed their curse on Ashar, his family, the house where they lived and the room where the massacre had taken place. Firaq Manzil was doomed from that moment onwards. It would never find peace again.

As sanity returned to Ashar and he struggled to gain control over his berserk mind, he looked at his own doing with horrified eyes. He had murdered his own daughter, whom he adored, and he had killed and mutilated a serving British army officer. The servants of the house, who had rushed to the scene of the mayhem, held his arms tightly, as he continued to rant and rave, ultimately collapsing, his body heaving with sobs, as he grieved for his daughter and the terrible tragedy that he had invited upon himself. He had no misgivings about what would happen now. Retribution would be swift - not only would he be arrested and hanged, it was entirely possible that his neighbours and his community too would face British wrath. His thoughts now under control, and under the counsel of his servants, it was decided to dig a shallow grave in a corner of the room where the tragedy had occurred. It would serve as a burial place for the unfortunate Aatifa. With the severed head lolling to one side, there was no way that she could be given a proper funeral and interred in a graveyard, as per the tenets of Islam. The hacked body of Reggie was carried to a corner behind the east wing of the property and set on fire with kerosene, to prevent identification. Ashar hoped that Reggie would not have confided to anyone about his clandestine visit to the old quarter of the city - an activity which was frowned upon by the colonial administration. But burning a human body, with limited resources, is not an easy job. Realising the futility of this exercise, it was decided to dump Reggie's partially burnt body into the unused well, and board it up. The room of the tragedy was cleaned, all traces of blood and struggle removed, and incense sticks burnt over the freshly dug grave of the unfortunate Aatifa. The floor stones were re-affixed over the spot; soon it would be impossible to identify that one corner of the room had been dug up, into which the mortal remains of a murdered young girl had been interred. The room was closed and locked. The gruesome events of the day came to close and the family servants were sworn to secrecy.

Aatifa had lost her mother at a very young age. It was Ashar who had raised her with all the love and affection that a single parent could provide. That night, Ashar could not sleep. He tossed and turned, trying to blank out his mind from re-living the horrors of the day. And as he drifted into an uneasy slumber, he thought that he could see his dead wife standing at the foot of his bed. She was as beautiful as ever, but her eyes were streaked with tears. The vision slowly faded and he could feel his own body wracked with sobs. But wait.. who was running on the veranda of the inner courtyard of this rambling house at this hour? From the pitter-patter, it appeared to be a young child. Someone giggled.. a sound he could immediately recognise as that of Aatifa, when she had been a child. But no.. Aatifa was not a child anymore, was she? She had grown up to become a beautiful young woman. And now Aatifa was dead; brutally killed. Her head severed from her body. She could not even have the *Salat al-Janazah* prayers recited for her after her death, such was her unfortunate fate - forced as she was to lie under paving stones, in an unmarked grave, inside a room of her own house.

Ashar continued to doze fitfully, his mind on the verge on insanity. Sometime during the night, he felt something glowering in the dark. He could sense two baleful eyes looking malevolently at him, even though his own eyelids were closed. The staring eyes were grey-green.. like the dead Reggie's eyes.. but Reggie was not there. Something was on fire. His bed, his own body. His bedclothes. There was fire everywhere. But it did not hurt. Nothing could hurt him anymore. He was like one possessed by an *ifrit*, a demon, which now controlled his actions and had him at his mercy.

IV

2020

A forest rest house, five kilometres away from Almora town, was to be the temporary home for Yusuf and his family. They had hurriedly left Firaq Manzil after the tragedy and had reached Almora after a tedious journey by train and road. Tahira had recovered from her shock, but appeared to be dull and listless after that incident. Yusuf and Fatima had unanimously decided that the ancestral house was not safe for them, whatever might be the reason. If Tahira had to stay away from her husband in any case, she could settle in Haldwani or Almora or even Dehra. But Lucknow was now out of question. Yusuf's cousins had agreed to dispatch his belongings as soon as some sort of permanent establishment had been finalised for Fatima and Tahira, after which Yusuf would re-join at Rikiyasain, his current place of posting. In the meantime, Yusuf had made up his mind to be constantly beside his family and assure them that the danger was gone.

The typical cottage-style rest house was cosy and sunny. Surrounded by tall trees and lush greenery, husband and wife felt secure and happy after a long hiatus. The full time cook-cum-chowkidar was a sturdy, affable fellow, who could rustle up simple meals without much ado, and also look after their day-to-day comforts. The young parents felt reassured and convinced that Tahira would soon recover from her trauma and become her cheerful self once more. The child, however, preferred to stay indoors, staring blankly in front of her. No longer playful or chirpy, she seemed to have acquired a new personality altogether.

One evening saw Yusuf and Fatima relaxing in the living room of the rest house. Tahira was nowhere to be seen. It was dark and forbidding outside, with clouds scudding across an overcast sky - signalling a sudden thunderstorm so characteristic of the hills. Desiring to have their daughter sit with them in the cosy confines of the living room, the young parents arose and entered their bedroom. Inside, they found Tahira sitting on a low chair; her eyes were blank, staring into space as she muttered to herself. She seemed to be talking unintelligibly to someone in low tones. This ghastly sight sent a shiver up the spines of husband and wife. Realising that Tahira had not yet recovered from her ordeal, Fatima rushed forward, lifting the child and hugging her to her breast. Tahira did not seem to recognise her mother; she remained limp like a lifeless doll.

Behind them, a glass of water kept on the corner table slowly moved to the edge on its own and toppled over, splashing its contents on the floor.

ЖЖЖ

Epilogue

The city of Lucknow and its surrounding areas can boast of having several graves and gravesites, both Muslim and British, located in some of the most unexpected locations and positioned at rather unconventional angles. The British graves at random places are understandable. During the tumultuous days of 1857 - 58, there was hardly any time for proper obsequies when European officers or soldiers died. With cannon balls and grapeshot whizzing past, all that the living could do was to hurriedly dump the bodies of their dead colleagues in shallow graves, and perhaps place a marker, so that the location could be pin-pointed at a later date. But such a stratagem did not work every time. For example, Mountstuart Jackson, his sisters, Madeleine and Georgina, Captain Patrick Orr and several others, who had earlier escaped from Sitapur, and had become captives of Begum Hazrat Mahal in Lucknow, had been later put to death by the revolutionaries and buried in an unspecified spot opposite the North East Gateway of Kaiserbagh. Later, the exact location of their mass grave proved to be an impossible task, and it was decided to just erect a pyramidal memorial, the "Orr Monument", designated for "Victims of 1857" - where it stands till today.

Lt. Augustus Otway Mayne was one of six brothers who were serving in the British Army at the time of the Indian Mutiny, only two of whom survived. Lieutenant Mayne served in the Bengal Horse Artillery. Killed on November 14, 1857, it was reported that his corpse was found by Field Marshal Roberts, who "took his dear friend Mayne out at early dawn and dug his grave and buried him in his blue frock-coat and riding boots and, as they laid him there, leant down and fixed his eyeglass into his eye as he always wore it in the heat of the fray." His now deteriorating grave lies on the seventh fairway at Lucknow Golf Course, being "a cause of great frustration to golfers." And not only that - the site is avoided by golfers (the general public does not have access to the site anyhow), as it is believed to be haunted by the wandering spirit of Mayne, who appears on horseback on moonlit nights.

Kothi Hayat Baksh, later christened as Major Bank's House and presently Raj Bhawan, is reportedly haunted by the ghost of Major Stephen Raikes Hodson, who had earned notoriety after he arrested Bahadur Shah Zafar and his family from Humayun's Tomb, Delhi on September 20, 1857, which he followed up by massacring the unarmed princes in full public view, the next day. Hodson's nemesis awaited him in Lucknow, when he was fatally wounded during the decisive battle at the Begum Kothi on March 12, 1858 (discussed later). He was carried to Kothi Hayat Baksh, where he died in great pain early next morning. His khaki-clad ghost is supposed to still

Fig. 13: The "Orr Monument" (1859), Robert and Harriet Tytler.

Fig. 14: Grave of Lt. AO Mayne Lucknow, Golf Club (2019), Alok Sharan.

Fig. 15: Grave of Major Hodson,
La Martiniere College Grounds, Unidentified Photographer

Fig. 16: Alambagh Kothi grounds with Havelock's unmarked grave under Mango Tree (1858), Felice Beato.

stalk the house and walk through the rooms of the building. Hodson's melancholy grave is extant today in the grounds of the La Martiniere College for Boys.

Fig. 17: Obelisk on Henry Havelock's grave (2019), Author.

Three hurriedly dug graves of British soldiers, Henry P Garvey, Act. Mate, Captain Halley Hutchinson and Sgt. S. Newman, exist within the premises of the Nawabi garden called Vilayati Bagh. Contrary to popular myth, none of these three fallen British soldiers were killed during any action within or near the Vilayati Bagh. Garvey was killed at Begum Kothi on March 11, 1858, whereas Hutchinson and Newman were killed in action at Musa Bagh on March 9 and March 19, 1858 respectively. Henry Havelock, Commander of the British forces against the Indian mutineers died of dysentery on November, 24, 1857 at Dilkusha, Lucknow. His body was carried to Alambagh, another Nawabi garden, and hurriedly buried in the open grounds, where there were three mango trees. The letter "H" was carved on the tree, whose branches shaded the makeshift grave. Later, an obelisk, with a plaque was erected on the spot by Havelock's son, Marshman Havelock. The Alambagh grounds were also used as a cemetery for other fallen British soldiers, including Lt. Henry Ayton, Lt. Dundas Gordon and others. In present times, the cemetery has vanished, but Havelock's grave and obelisk remain within a small enclosure. Fortunately, there is no reported haunting in the area, either by Havelock or his fellow soldiers, although the premises are now a densely populated residential area, with many of the graves having being indiscriminately uprooted and scattered.

A British officer, Captain Frederick Wale (the eighth son of General Charles Wale of Shelford), who was in command of the 1st Sikh Irregular Cavalry, had been fatally injured and who subsequently died on March 21, 1858. He was buried in the premises of Musa Bagh within an enclosure, erected by one Captain LB Jones, Acting Commandant, 1st Sikh Irregular Cavalry, as a token of regard for his officer, whom he admired both as a soldier and a friend. Fortunately, Wale is not known to be a restless spirit wandering about in the desolate ruins of Musa Bagh, but as a *saint*. As an act of reverence, (or blind faith), the locals offer wine, meat and even cigarettes on the now *mazar* (grave of a Muslim religious leader or saint) of Captain Wale, reverently called *Kaptan Shah Baba*, *Gore Baba* and *Cigarette Wale Baba*, with the hope that their wishes might be fulfilled by the benevolent *baba*.

The slow and steady deterioration of British graves, attributed to natural factors and insufficient upkeep, as well as instances of desecration, is understandable, considering the ethos and the resentment of the local public against their erstwhile colonial masters. However, it is somewhat alarming that entire cemeteries have, in some instances, been repurposed for residential or commercial development. The Archaeological Survey of India, New Delhi in a communication (F.No.T-19044/1/2019-M dt. May 25, 2019) listed the centrally protected monuments / sites under the jurisdiction of Lucknow Circle, which also detailed the various British cemeteries scattered in and around Lucknow, including Jahraila Road, Bargawan, Alambagh, Dilkusha, Gaughat, Kaiser Pasand (Kaiserbagh), near "Fort Machhi Bhavan", Raja Incha Singh Compound, La Martiniere grounds, Vilayat (*sic*) Bagh, Kalan-ki-Lat (*sic*), Lucknow-Rae Bareilly Road, Lucknow-Faizabad Road, Lucknow-Kanpur Road, Marion (*sic*) and Chiria Jhil (*sic*). This was despite the fact that the Ministry of Culture, Govt of India had already listed the Gaughat and Jahraila as "missing", *vide* notification dt. January 2, 2018, by the Press Information Bureau, Govt. of India. This indicated that some protected monuments (including cemeteries) existed only on paper. On the ground level, it is common knowledge in Lucknow that the Chiria Jheel, Kalan-ki-Lat and other cemeteries and graves have long disappeared due to rapid urbanisation and rampant encroachment, although they continue to exist on paper.

Fig. 18: The "Lat Kallan ki Lat" towering above a warren of shanties (2015), Oliver Frederick.

John Ulrich Collins joined the East India Company's Bengal Infantry in 1770, rising to the rank of Major after twenty-four years' service. A year later he became Resident at Gwalior, in the court of Daulat Rao Scindia. Nick-named as 'King Collins', due to his imperious nature, he remained a bachelor all his life and had a short stint as Resident at Lucknow (1806-07). He died suddenly on June 18, 1807 and was buried in a cemetery near Kaiserbagh and a 60 feet high obelisk was erected in his memory by Sa'adat Ali Khan (sixth Nawab of Awadh), which came to be locally known as *Lat Kallan ki Lat*, being the tallest free standing structure of Lucknow at one point of time. The cemetery is no longer identifiable although the obelisk continues to stand tall among a warren of tightly packed shanties. Thankfully, no supernatural activities have been reported in the area, where a British entire cemetery was gobbled up, with scant regard for the law. This now vanished British cemetery had another claim to fame. Not only the mortal remains of Col. Richard Wilcox, Royal Astronomer of Taaron Wali Kothi built by King Nasir-ud-Din Haider lay buried there, Rev. H. Kirwan, the Chaplain of Lucknow, who joined in 1852, forbade some burials in the consecrated grounds, because they were Protestants or Baptists, and not Catholics. In one instance, the body of a dead child began to decompose because of all this controversy, and it took the personal intervention of the then Resident, William Sleeman, for the burial to finally take place.

Other than regular mausolea, isolated Muslim graves also appear in Lucknow and its environs, in the oddest of locations, placed at various angles. Many have assumed the status of *mazars*, acquiring cult status over a period of time, and periodic religious festivities connected to these are not uncommon. Once such *mazar* in the Lucknow Residency premises has already been discussed in one story (*The Lovelorn Ghost*). It is common knowledge that due respect and devotion has to be given to these graves / *mazars*, otherwise unpleasant consequences are the norm. Even the British took cognisance of the religious connotations of these, and generally took care not to disturb these graves to the extent possible, during the landscaping of the city post 1857. A well-known example of this is the *mazar* of Khamman Peer Baba, located on one end of the Charbagh Railway Station at

Lucknow. British engineers were unable to successfully lay the tracks in the vicinity, during the construction of the new railway station in 1920, till such time that on local advice, the tracks were shifted away from the *mazar*, incurring extra cost. The British were also constrained to allow devotees to enter the station, without platform tickets on Thursdays - a day considered to be auspicious for paying respects to the holy man, and seek grant of boons. The *mazars* of Sheikh Qawam-ud-din and Shah Mina, Sufi saints, whose arrival pre-dated the Nawabi rule of Lucknow continue to exist in the premises of the Medical College (now University) and were not disturbed during its construction.

As discussed above, if such a grave is located in one's vicinity, whether the grave is of an identified "saint" or even an anonymous person, then proper regard and respect have to be extended to it, if one wants a peaceful existence, or even wants his business to flourish. A particular location in Mahanagar area, with mixed use for residential and commercial purposes proved to be quite inauspicious and no shop / cafe / showroom / lounge would succeed in its vicinity. Contiguous to the place, a huge banyan tree existed, under which there was a grave of an unknown person. The grave was not even visible, although the locals were aware of its past existence. Burning a light on a designated spot on Thursdays, seemed to have placated the agitated spirit whose grave was being disturbed due to

Fig. 19: Gravestone of Lt. Charles Dashwood (2021), Author.

commercial activities. A similar tale of a particular spot near present day Janpath Market is well known, which just could not succeed for any commercial venture, despite its prime location. Janpath Market was built on the ruins of the Begum Kothi, where hundreds of Indian freedom fighters had died on a single day, while defending the city against British aggressors. William Forbes-Mitchell (1910), writing his memoirs in *Reminiscences of the Great Mutiny 1857-59*, has given a graphic account of the assault on Begum Kothi. According to him, "by evening, eight hundred and sixty of the enemy lay dead in the center court alone, and many hundreds more were killed in the different enclosures and buildings. When daylight broke in the morning of March 12, 1858, the sight was horrible as there were hundreds of bodies all around, some still burning and some half-burnt, and the stench was sickening."

The Noor Baksh Kothi, present residence of the District Magistrate of Lucknow has a similar sinister reputation. Built by Sa'adat Ali Khan, the sixth Nawab of Awadh, it is purported that within the Kothi are some Muslim graves in a room under the main staircase. The graves pre-dated the Kothi, and were not disturbed during the construction of the latter. It has been reported that the room containing the graves is reportedly opened and cleaned every Thursday, followed by lighting of incense sticks, in a bid to pacify the restless spirits in the room.

The ghostly ruins of Dilkusha continue to exist today for all to see. Built as a Nawabi hunting lodge by Sa'adat Ali Khan and modelled on an English manor called Seaton Delavel in Northumberland, England, it was partially demolished by the British due to unspecified reasons, after the revolution of 1857 - 58 was already over. The grounds of Dilkusha also have the graves of Lieutenant William Paul, 4th Punjab Rifles, and Lieutenant Charles Keith Dashwood, of the 18th B.N.I. Lt. Paul, born in Elgin and 29 years of age had sustained wounds on November 16, 1857 during the assault on Sikandar Bagh, and had died on the following day. Charles Keith Dashwood was 19 years old when the siege of Lucknow began. Described as "a nice boy, a great favourite with every one, and such a tall handsome fellow", he fought in the defence in the Lucknow Residency, but accidentally shot himself while cleaning his gun; the wound was not fatal and he was back on duty soon after. On the 4th of November, however, while making sketches of the Residency grounds, Charles was struck by round shot and lost both his legs. He died at the Dilkusha on November 22, 1857, where he had been carried on a *doolie* (palanquin), after the evacuation of the Lucknow Residency was over. He was only 19 years old then, and the movement had been too much for him.

Thus, the living and the dead continue to co-exist peacefully in the city of Lucknow today, with neither disturbing the other, excepting in rare circumstances.

Suggested Readings

Ahmed, Rollo, *The Black Art* (1994), Senate, London.

Bond, Ruskin, *A Face In The Dark* (2004), Penguin, New Delhi.

Bond, Ruskin, *Ghost Stories from the Raj* (2002), Rupa, New Delhi.

Brunton, Paul, *A Search in Secret India* (1934), Rider, London.

Croker, BM, *To Let* (1906), JB Lippincott, Philadelphia, USA.

Croker, BM and Perrin, Alice, *The Dread of Night* (2023), Speaking Tiger, New Delhi.

Crooke, W, *An Introduction To The Popular Religion And Folklore of Northern India* (1894), Government Press, Allahabad.

Finkel, Irving, *The First Ghosts - Most Ancient of Legacies* (2021), Hodder & Stoughton, London.

Frazer, JG, *The Golden Bough: A Study in Magic and Religion* (2009), Oxford University Press, London.

MacLure, Harry, *Dark Nights and Eerie Shadows - Ghostly Anglo-Indian Tales* (2019), Anglo-Ink, Chennai.

Mukherjee, S, *The Book of Indian Ghost Stories* - reprint from the original, published in 1914 (2010), Scholastic, New Delhi.

Perrin, Alice, *East of Suez: Tales of Love, Betrayal and Haunting from the Raj* (2015), Speaking Tiger, New Delhi.

Ray, Satyajit (*auth.*) and Majumdar, Gopa (*trans.*), *Classic Satyajit Ray* (2012), Penguin, New Delhi.

Raza, Moosa, *Of Nawabs and Nightingales & Other Episodes* (1995), Rupa, New Delhi.

Samanta, Suchitra (*ed.*), *Hauntings* (2000), Katha, New Delhi.

Sarkar, PC, *Lucknow - Buildings, Begums and The British* (2015), Kalpaz, Delhi.

Sarkar, PC, *Lucknow - Ode To A City* (2021), Kalpaz, Delhi.

Sarkar, PC, *Abode Of Fairies - Lucknow's Parikhana* (2022), Kalpaz, Delhi.

Sarkar, PC, *Lucknow Chronicles: Memories, Musings, Myths* (2023), Kalpaz, Delhi.

Sarkar, PC, *Colonial Lucknow, Burra Sahib and Chota Hazry* (2024) Kalpaz, Delhi.

Svobod, Robert, *Aghora: At The Left Hand of God* (1993), Rupa, New Delhi.

Swamy, KRN and Ravi, M (*eds.*), *British Ghosts and Occult India* (2004), Writers Workshop, Kolkata.

Talha, Parveen, *Fida-e-Lucknow: Tales of The City and Its People* (2013), Niyogi, New Delhi.

Wheatley, Dennis, *The Devil and All His Works* (1971), Arrow Books, London.

Wilson, Colin, *Poltergeist! A Study in Destructive Haunting* (1981), Hodder & Stoughton, London.